HOW TO START A CONSULTING CAREER

A Comprehensive Guide to Building And Scaling Your Consulting Dream In To Reality

Jeanelle K. Douglas

Copyright © 2024 by Jeanelle K. Douglas. All rights reserved. No part of this book, HOW TO START A CONSULTING CAREER, may be reproduced, stored in a retrieval system, or transmitted in any form or by any means, electronic, mechanical, photocopying, recording, or otherwise, without the prior written permission of the author, Jeanelle K. Douglas.

Table of Contents

Introduction 7
    Defining consulting 9
    Why choose a career in consulting? 11
    An Overview of the Book 14

Understanding consulting 17
    Types of consulting 21
    Skills and traits required for success 23
    Preparing to Work in Consulting 26
    Assessing Your Skills and Interests 28
    Educational Background and Certifications 31
    Gaining relevant experience 35

Creating Your Consulting Toolkit 38
Developing analytical and problem-solving skills. ... 41
    Communication and Presentation Skills. 44
    Networking and Relationship Building 47
    Develop your Consulting Brand 50
    Define your niche and expertise 52

- Creating a Personal Brand 54
- Creating an Online Presence. 56
- Finding Your First Client 58
- Leveraging Your Network 61
- Market and promote your services. 63
- Pitch and Proposals 67

Providing Exceptional Consulting Services 70
- Establishing Client Relationships. 74
- Managing Projects Effectively 77
- Handling Challenges and Difficult Clients 81

Scaling Your Consulting Business 83
- Hiring Support Staff 87
- Expanding your service offerings 92
- Scaling your operations 94

Navigating the Consulting Industry 99
- Staying current on industry trends 101
- Developing Strategies To Effectively Compete In The Market . 105
- Continuing professional development is essential 109
- Consultation ethics and professionalism 112
- Upholding Ethical Standards. 114

Managing Conflicts of Interest 118

Ensuring Client Confidentiality. 120

Manage your consulting career 122

Setting Goals and Milestones. 125

Balancing work and personal life. 128

Continuous Learning And Growth. 130

Conclusion 132

Final thoughts 133

Next Steps on Your Consulting Journey 135

Sample consulting agreements 139

A Glossary of Consulting Terms. 141

THIS PAGE IS LEFT INTENTIONALLY.

GO GRAB YOUR WRITING PAD FOR NOTE KEEPING, YOU ARE ABOUT TO GET THE BEST SECRET TO UNLEASH YOUR NEW CAREER AS A CONSLUTANT.

Introduction

Embarking on a career as a consultant is analogous to setting sail on an adventurous trip into the domain of problem-solving, strategy development, and revolutionary change. Whether you're inclined to management consulting, financial advising, IT consulting, or any other specialized profession, the route to becoming a successful consultant is as diverse as the hurdles you'll meet along the way.

In this book, we dig into the complexity of this dynamic industry, giving insights, tactics, and practical guidance to equip aspiring consultants like you to navigate the path ahead with confidence and purpose.

Consulting is not only a profession; it's a mindset—a dedication to continual learning, adaptation, and the tireless pursuit of greatness. It's about utilizing your skills to produce real influence for clients, organizations, and communities. Whether you're a new graduate exploring career alternatives or a seasoned professional seeking a fresh challenge, the consulting industry beckons with infinite potential for growth and fulfillment.

Throughout this book, we'll study the fundamental concepts of consulting, from understanding the many forms of consulting and honing critical skills to building your own brand and finding your first customers. We'll dig into the details of delivering outstanding consulting services, expanding your firm, and navigating the challenges of the consulting sector with integrity and professionalism.

Drawing on real-world experiences, best practices, and timeless advice from seasoned consultants, "How to Start a Career as a Consultant" serves as your indispensable handbook on this transforming path. Whether you wish to begin your solo consultancy, join a prominent business, or carve yourself a niche in a specialized subject, this book offers you the skills, insights, and tactics to chart your route and handle the obstacles and possibilities that lie ahead.

So, if you're ready to begin a successful career as a consultant, let's go on this revolutionary adventure together.

Start on your journey and discover the vast opportunities in the world of consulting.

Defining consulting

Imagine becoming the go-to problem solver, the trusted advisor, and the catalyst for change in both big and small firms. That's the core of consulting, a dynamic and complex profession that allows individuals to have a concrete effect on the world around them. In the world of consulting, your experience becomes your currency, and your ability to manage complicated issues and offer unique solutions sets you apart. Whether you're offering strategic advice to Fortune 500 corporations, helping startups optimize their business models, or supporting non-profits in fulfilling their purpose, consulting is about utilizing your unique talents and experience to achieve good change.

But consulting is more than simply delivering advice; it's about learning the specifics of your customers' businesses, finding their pain areas, and partnering with them to build personalized plans for success. It's about asking the appropriate questions, challenging traditional thinking, and helping your customers transform solutions. As you embark on your journey to start a career as a consultant, defining consulting becomes not simply a question of knowing a profession, but embracing a mindset—an approach to problem-solving that is as creative as it is analytical and as strategic as it is empathic.

In this book, we go deep into the core of consulting, exploring its complexities, its problems, and its infinite promise. From mastering the art of communication to polishing your analytical abilities, from creating your own brand to navigating the subtleties of client relationships, this book is your passport to success in the world of consulting.

So, if you're ready to unlock your potential, make a difference, and build yourself a profession that's as gratifying as it is influential, join us on this amazing trip into the world of consulting. The adventure awaits, and the possibilities are boundless.

Why choose a career in consulting?

Choosing a career in consulting involves embracing a lifestyle characterized by ongoing learning, diverse challenges, and the opportunity to make a meaningful impact. Whether you're a fresh graduate exploring your possibilities or a seasoned professional seeking a new challenge, the consulting business provides a plethora of compelling reasons to choose it as your career path.

1. **Range and Diversity:** One of the most tempting parts of a career in consulting is the sheer range of projects and customers you'll meet. From advising large organizations to cooperating with startups, every day brings a new chance to solve fresh difficulties, learn about numerous sectors, and enhance your skill set.
2. **Continuous Learning:** Consulting is a profession that thrives on intellectual curiosity and the quest for information. Consultants continually encounter fresh ideas, developing trends, and cutting-edge technology. This ongoing learning not only makes the work intriguing but also ensures that you're always developing and improving in your profession.
3. **Professional Development:** Consulting businesses spend extensively on the development of their workers, providing extensive training programs, mentorship opportunities, and tools to assist their advancement. Whether it's sharpening your analytical abilities, perfecting the art of communication, or

building experience in a certain area, consulting gives various options for professional growth.

4. **Impactful Work:** Consultants have the luxury of working on projects that have a demonstrable influence on enterprises, organizations, and even society as a whole. Whether it's helping a struggling firm turn its fortunes around, advising a non-profit on how to optimize its influence, or guiding a government agency through a significant transition, the work of consultants typically leads to real and enduring change.

5. **Global Possibilities:** With the potential to engage with clients and teams from all over the world, the consulting sector is fundamentally global. This worldwide experience not only broadens your viewpoint but also provides opportunities for new initiatives and cooperation across boundaries.

6. Consulting appeals to individuals with an entrepreneurial mindset who excel in dynamic environments, enjoy tackling new challenges, and are unafraid to innovate. Whether you're working for a huge consulting business or beginning your own practice, consulting gives you lots of opportunity to express your entrepreneurial spirit and ambition.

7. **Highly Rewarding:** In addition to delivering attractive wages and benefits, consulting is a career that rewards performance and outcomes. As you help your customers solve complicated challenges, achieve their goals, and drive development, you'll

enjoy a great sense of pleasure and fulfillment in knowing that your work has made a meaningful impact.

8. **Networking and Relationships:** Consulting gives you unmatched chances to create a large network of connections, both inside your business and among clients and industry peers. These partnerships not only improve your work life but also provide doors to future career prospects and collaborations.

In short, a career in consulting offers a unique mix of intellectual challenge, professional progress, and significant influence that few other occupations can equal. Consulting offers a diverse and satisfying career path for individuals attracted to project variety, continuous learning opportunities, and the chance to make a difference in the world.

An Overview of the Book

Welcome to the exploration of a transforming trip—a voyage into the dynamic and complex world of consulting. Within the pages of this book, we embark on an expedition that goes beyond the typical confines of career guidance, digging deep into the core of what it means to establish a career as a consultant.

Our trip begins by unraveling the very core of consulting, providing a vivid image of a profession that extends beyond the normal confines of employment. We dig into the art and science of consulting, where experience becomes a commodity and the capacity to unravel complicated situations transforms individuals into trusted advisors, problem solvers, and architects of change.

This book isn't just a manual; it's a compass, leading you through the unexplored frontiers of a career in consulting. As we walk through the pages, you'll get insights into the complexities of this dynamic profession—comprehending the different elements of consulting, from strategic management counsel to specialist sector knowledge. The chapters evolve organically, matching the stages of your own professional progress. We start with the foundation, analyzing the underlying attributes that create a successful consultant. It's about polishing not only technical abilities but also growing the art of effective communication, critical thinking, and flexibility—attributes that set consultants apart in a world of ever-evolving difficulties.

We venture further into the realm of personal branding. In a career where individual expertise is crucial, we educate you on developing a story that defines your specialization, establishes your knowledge, and connects with the clients you wish to serve. This isn't just about developing a brand; it's about becoming a trusted and recognizable force in your chosen sector.

Our adventure takes a realistic turn as we confront the hurdles of getting those elusive first clients. Drawing from the experiences of others who have navigated similar waters before you, we cover the subtleties of networking, marketing, and the delicate art of making compelling ideas that fascinate and persuade. But this isn't a basic guide to getting projects; it's an expedition into the core of client relationships. We address the art of not only meeting expectations but exceeding them—how to create trust, manage projects efficiently, and traverse the tricky terrain of varied client personalities and expectations.

As the story evolves, we enter the realm of scalability. It's not only about managing projects; it's about developing a sustainable and flourishing consulting firm. We cover the methods for expansion, the art of recruiting and mentoring, and the difficult balance between extending your services and preserving the quality that characterizes your firm.

In the ever-evolving environment of the consulting sector, we address the significance of staying ahead of the curve. We navigate the currents of market developments, competitiveness, and the need for continuous learning. The trip isn't just about achieving a goal; it's about changing, adapting, and succeeding in a field that demands nothing less than greatness.

Ethics and professionalism become our guiding lights as we dig into the duties that come with the title of consultant. It's about more than simply delivering advice; it's about preserving ethical standards, keeping integrity, and safeguarding the confidence that clients invest in your knowledge.

As we complete our journey, we reflect on the comprehensive picture of a consulting career. It's not just a job; it's a lifestyle. We examine the delicate dance of setting objectives, accomplishing milestones, and maintaining equilibrium in the ebb and flow of professional life. This handbook isn't a prescriptive guidebook; it's a companion, sharing insights, wisdom, and practical counsel from people who have traveled the route before you. Stories of victories and tribulations weave a tapestry that resonates with the pulse of the consulting profession. So, welcome to a voyage of self-discovery, growth, and change—an excursion into the realm of consulting, where each page uncovers a new chapter in your own tale of success. May this book be your compass, your confidante, and your source of inspiration as you embark on the thrilling path of establishing a career as a consultant.

Understanding consulting

Embarking on a career in consulting is analogous to walking into a domain where every obstacle provides an opportunity, every problem a puzzle to solve, and every client a chance to make a meaningful contribution. Before getting into the nuances of how to start a career as a consultant, it's vital to comprehend the underlying essence of consulting itself.

Consulting, at its foundation, is about offering professional advice and counsel to individuals, businesses, organizations, or even governments to help them solve complicated issues, make strategic decisions, and accomplish their goals. It's a job that involves a unique combination of talents, expertise, and mentality, where consultants function as trusted advisors, strategists, and change agents.

In the context of establishing a career as a consultant, knowing the complex nature of consulting is vital. It's not only about delivering answers; it's about recognizing the complexities of diverse sectors, markets, and organizational dynamics. Consultants need to acquire a thorough awareness of their customers' difficulties, goals, and aspirations and customize their approach appropriately.

Consulting spans a wide range of fields and expertise, from management consulting and financial advice to technology consulting and beyond. Each field of consulting comes with its own set of difficulties, opportunities, and best practices, forcing consultants to consistently adapt and grow their skill set to be relevant in a quickly changing world.

Effective consultants possess a unique blend of analytical, problem-solving, and communication abilities. They thrive at analyzing difficult challenges, discovering core causes, and providing imaginative and realistic solutions. Effective communication is also crucial, since consultants must be able to present their ideas, insights, and recommendations effectively and persuasively to clients and stakeholders. But maybe what truly sets consultants apart is their ability to negotiate ambiguity and uncertainty with confidence and grace. Consulting typically entails dealing with insufficient information, unclear challenges, and a variety of parties with opposing interests. As a result, consultants must be comfortable functioning in situations marked by uncertainty, ambiguity, and rapid change and exhibit adaptability and resilience to succeed in such contexts.

Understanding consulting is about seeing it as a dynamic and varied profession that demands a particular combination of skills, knowledge, and perspective. It's about embracing the difficulties and possibilities that come with helping customers solve complicated situations and achieve their goals. And when prospective consultants embark on their journey to establish a career in consulting, this knowledge serves as the foundation upon which they can grow their expertise, polish their talents, and make a real difference in the field of consulting.

One of the key tasks of consultants is to undertake extensive studies of their customers' businesses or projects. This entails obtaining and analyzing data, finding relevant trends and patterns, and diagnosing underlying concerns or opportunities. Consultants employ a number of analytical techniques and processes to unearth insights that shape their suggestions and plans.

Once equipped with insights, consultants work closely with their customers to design and implement strategies that suit their individual goals and objectives. This may entail formulating corporate strategies, reforming organizational procedures, deploying new technology, or starting marketing campaigns, among other things. Consultants act as partners with their customers, supporting them through the process of change and transformation.

In addition to offering strategic guidance, consultants also play a significant role in project management and implementation. They ensure that projects stay on track, meet deadlines, and achieve objectives. Consultants may engage with cross-functional teams within their client businesses or interact with external suppliers and partners to produce results.

Communication is another crucial part of a consultant's function. Consultants must be skilled communicators, capable of presenting complicated concepts and suggestions in a clear, succinct, and convincing manner. Whether presenting results to top executives, organizing workshops with frontline staff, or producing reports for clients, consultants must excel at communicating with stakeholders at all levels of a company.

Ultimately, what consultants do is about creating a visible influence on their customers' businesses and helping them accomplish their goals. It's about utilizing knowledge, creativity, and strategic thinking to achieve good change and transformation. And as you embark on your journey to start a career in consulting, knowing the diverse and powerful nature of what consultants do will serve as your compass, guiding you towards success in this dynamic and fulfilling field.

Types of consulting

As you begin your road to establishing a career in consulting, it's crucial to grasp the diverse terrain of consulting and the numerous sorts of consulting practices that exist. Consulting is not a one-size-fits-all career; rather, it comprises a wide range of specialties and niches, each with its own unique set of difficulties, opportunities, and skill sets.

Management consulting is one of the most popular forms of consultancy. Management consultants work with organizations of all kinds, from small enterprises to major corporations, to help them improve their performance and accomplish their strategic objectives. This may entail performing organizational evaluations, establishing strategic plans, executing change management efforts, or advising on mergers and acquisitions.

Financial consulting is another popular type of consultancy. Financial consultants provide specialized advice and counsel to customers on money-related issues, such as investment management, financial planning, risk assessment, and valuation. Financial consultants may work with people, corporations, or government organizations to help them make educated financial decisions and accomplish their financial goals.

Technology consulting is also an important component of the consulting industry. Technology consultants advise companies on how to use technology to improve operations, create innovation, and gain a competitive advantage. This might include building and deploying IT systems, consulting on cybersecurity measures, or creating digital transformation initiatives.

Another common type of consulting is strategy consulting, which helps customers develop and implement strategic plans to achieve long-term goals. Strategy consultants help firms examine market possibilities, identify growth areas, and build plans to profit from them. This may include market research, competition analysis, and strategic planning.

In addition to these major forms of consulting, there are several specialized consulting firms that focus on certain sectors or areas of expertise. Healthcare consulting, for example, advises healthcare firms on healthcare delivery, patient care, and regulatory compliance. Environmental consulting focuses on providing guidance on environmental issues such as pollution management, sustainability, and regulatory compliance.

As you explore a career in consulting, you should research the various types of consulting practices and find those that match your interests, talents, and career objectives. Understanding the many forms of consulting can help you make educated decisions regarding your career path and position within the consulting sector, whether you are interested in management consulting, financial consulting, technology consulting, or another specialized field.

Skills and traits required for success

It is critical to understand that success in this dynamic and tough field necessitates a certain set of talents, attributes, and characteristics. Consulting is more than just providing professional advice or developing new solutions; it is about developing connections, negotiating complicated issues, and achieving significant change. Let's look at some of the important talents and characteristics required for success in consulting.

First and foremost, clear communication is essential. As a consultant, you'll need to communicate complicated ideas, insights, and suggestions to clients, stakeholders, and teammates. Clear and succinct communication is vital when presenting results to top executives, leading workshops with frontline employees, or writing reports for customers. Strong verbal, written, and interpersonal communication skills are essential for establishing trust, encouraging cooperation, and ensuring that your message connects with your target audience.

Consulting success also requires analytical thinking and problem-solving skills. Consultants are responsible for unraveling difficult problems, detecting underlying concerns, and finding innovative and practical solutions. This necessitates the capacity to think critically, evaluate data, see patterns and trends, and reach meaningful conclusions. Strong analytical abilities are required to make educated judgments and drive results, whether conducting market research, financial analysis, or designing operational strategy.

Flexibility is another important quality for success in consulting. Consulting is a fast-paced, ever-changing environment in which customers' needs, market conditions, and project requirements can change quickly. Consultants must be able to swiftly adjust to changing conditions, handle ambiguity and uncertainty, and maintain an agile attitude. This necessitates adaptability, resilience, and a willingness to accept new challenges and opportunities as they emerge.

Collaboration are also essential for success in consulting. Consultants frequently work in interdisciplinary teams, collaborating with colleagues from various backgrounds and expertise areas to deliver results for clients. Effective teamwork necessitates strong interpersonal skills, active listening, and a willingness to share knowledge and experience. Building and maintaining positive working relationships with team members and clients is critical to achieving shared objectives and driving success.

Client management and relationship-building skills are also important for consulting success. Consultants must be able to connect with clients, understand their needs and goals, and establish trust and credibility through their actions and recommendations. This requires active listening, empathy, and the ability to anticipate and address client concerns and priorities. Building strong client relationships is critical for securing repeat business, generating referrals, and achieving long-term success in consulting.

Finally, success in consulting requires a strong desire to learn and grow professionally. The consulting industry is constantly evolving, with new technologies, methodologies, and best practices appearing at a rapid pace. To remain competitive in the marketplace, consultants must commit to continuous learning, staying up-to-date on industry trends, and expanding their knowledge and expertise. This necessitates a growth mindset, curiosity, and a willingness to pursue new opportunities for learning and development.

Success in consulting necessitates a wide range of skills, traits, and qualities, including effective communication, analytical thinking, adaptability, collaboration, client management, and a desire to learn and grow professionally. As you embark on your journey to a consulting career, cultivating these skills and traits will lay the groundwork for your success and meaningful impact in the dynamic and rewarding world of consulting.

Preparing to Work in Consulting

Preparing for a career in consulting is similar to laying the groundwork for a skyscraper; it necessitates meticulous planning, strategic thinking, and a solid framework to support your goals. There are several important steps you can take to position yourself for success in the dynamic and competitive world of consulting.

First and foremost, assess your skills, interests, and strengths. Consider your academic background, work experience, and extracurricular activities to identify areas where you excel and areas where you could improve further. Consider the distinct qualities and attributes you bring to the table, such as strong analytical skills, effective communication abilities, or a talent for problem solving.

Next, gain valuable experience and expertise in your chosen field. This may include pursuing internships, co-op placements, or part-time positions in consulting-related industries or functional areas. Gaining hands-on experience in real-world settings will not only improve your skills and knowledge, but it will also demonstrate to potential employers your dedication and passion for the consulting profession.

Invest in your education and career development. Consider pursuing advanced degrees, certifications, or specialized training programs to improve your credentials and broaden your knowledge in consulting-related fields. Whether it's getting an MBA, earning a professional certification in a specific industry or functional area, or attending workshops and seminars, continuous learning and professional development are critical for remaining competitive in the consulting industry.

Networking is another important part of preparing for a career in consulting. Take advantage of networking opportunities to meet professionals in the consulting industry, such as alumni, mentors, and experts. Attend industry conferences, networking events, and career fairs to broaden your professional network and learn about the consulting profession. Building meaningful relationships with industry professionals can lead to valuable opportunities such as informational interviews, job referrals, and future career prospects.

Establish your personal brand and online presence. In today's digital age, having a strong personal brand and a professional online presence can help you gain visibility and credibility in the consulting industry. Create a polished LinkedIn profile that highlights your skills, experiences, and accomplishments, and join consulting-related online communities and forums. Share thought leadership content, take part in discussions, and demonstrate your expertise to establish yourself as a credible and influential voice in the industry.

Finally, as you progress in your consulting career, cultivate a growth mindset and an openness to new challenges and opportunities. The consulting industry is dynamic and ever-changing, requiring consultants to respond quickly to new environments, technologies, and client needs. Maintaining a positive attitude, seeking out new learning opportunities, and embracing continuous growth and development will set you up for long-term success and fulfillment in the exciting and rewarding world of consulting.

Assessing Your Skills and Interests

Starting a consulting career is about more than just finding a job; it's about matching your passions, interests, and skills to the demands and expectations of the consulting industry. Before diving into the world of consulting, you should take a step back and evaluate your own capabilities, strengths, and areas for improvement.

Begin by reflecting on your academic background and professional experiences. Consider which courses, projects, or assignments you excelled at and enjoyed the most. What subjects or topics piqued your interest or sparked your curiosity? Identifying your academic strengths, whether they are in analytical courses like statistics or finance, problem-solving courses like operations management, or strategic courses like marketing or business strategy, can provide valuable insights into areas where you may excel in consulting.

Next, assess your professional experience and extracurricular activities. Consider the roles or projects where you demonstrated leadership, collaboration, and initiative. What were your responsibilities, and what did you accomplish? Whether you're leading a team project, organizing a fundraising event, or participating in a volunteer initiative, your professional experiences can reveal important information about your skills, interests, and areas of expertise that are transferable to consulting.

Also consider your soft skills and personal characteristics. Are you an effective communicator who can express ideas and concepts clearly and persuasively? Are you a critical thinker who can analyze problems, identify underlying causes, and devise novel solutions? Are you adaptable and resilient, able to thrive in fast-paced and constantly changing environments? These soft skills and personal qualities are just as important as technical skills in the consulting industry because they help you collaborate effectively, navigate challenges, and deliver results for clients.

Examine your interests and passions outside of academic and professional settings. What hobbies, activities, or causes are you passionate about? Whether it's volunteering for a nonprofit organization, participating in sports or artistic pursuits, or performing community service, your extracurricular activities can provide valuable insights into your values, motivations, and areas of interest, which can help you make career decisions in consulting.

Finally, seek feedback and advice from mentors, peers, and consulting industry experts. Contact people who are currently working in consulting or have experience in the field, and ask for their thoughts and opinions. Share with them your career aspirations, goals, and concerns, and ask for feedback on your skills, interests, and potential fit for a career in consulting. Their advice and support can help you navigate your career path and make informed decisions about pursuing a career in consulting.

Assessing your skills and interests is an important first step in pursuing a consulting career. Reflecting on your academic background, work experiences, soft skills, personal qualities, and extracurricular interests can provide you with valuable insights into your strengths, weaknesses, and areas for development, allowing you to make more informed career decisions and position yourself for success in the dynamic and rewarding consulting world.

Educational Background and Certifications

When it comes to starting a consulting career, your educational background and certifications can have a significant impact on your success. While there is no one-size-fits-all approach to consulting education, establishing a strong educational foundation and obtaining relevant certifications can significantly improve your credibility, expertise, and marketability in the consulting industry.

Many aspiring consultants pursue undergraduate or graduate degrees in business, economics, finance, management, engineering, or other disciplines.

These programs give students a thorough understanding of key business concepts, analytical frameworks, and problem-solving techniques that are required for success in consulting. Furthermore, some universities offer specialized programs or concentrations in consulting or management consulting, providing students with targeted coursework and hands-on learning opportunities in the consulting industry.

Obtaining advanced degrees in a relevant field, such as a Master of Business Administration (MBA) or a Master of Science (MS), can help you advance your career and open up new opportunities in consulting. MBA programs, in particular, are well-regarded in the consulting industry because they provide students with a broad-based business education, specialized coursework in areas such as strategy, operations, and finance, and valuable networking opportunities with industry professionals and graduates.

In addition to formal education, obtaining relevant certifications can help to strengthen your credentials and demonstrate your expertise in specific areas of consulting. Obtaining certifications such as the Chartered Management Consultant (ChMC), Certified Management Consultant (CMC), or Certified Business Consultant (CBC) can help validate your consulting skills, knowledge, and ethical standards. Professional associations and organizations, such as the Institute of Management Consultants (IMC) and the International Council of Management Consulting Institutes (ICMCI), offer these certifications, which typically require candidates to meet specific education, experience, and examination requirements.

Obtaining certifications in specialized areas such as project management, data analytics, or industry-specific domains can help you stand out from other candidates in the consulting industry.

Certifications such as Project Management Professional (PMP), Certified Analytics Professional (CAP), or industry-specific certifications in areas such as healthcare, finance, or information technology can help you demonstrate your expertise and position yourself as a subject matter expert in your chosen field.

Your educational background and certifications provide a solid foundation for your consulting career. By obtaining a solid education in relevant disciplines, pursuing advanced degrees, and obtaining relevant certifications. This will position you can improve your expertise, credibility, and marketability in the consulting industry, positioning yourself for success in this dynamic and rewarding field.

Aside from formal education and certifications, there are several other ways to improve your knowledge and skills in preparation for a career in consulting. Participation in workshops, seminars, and professional development programs provided by consulting firms, industry associations, and educational institutions is one such option. These programs offer valuable opportunities to learn from industry experts, gain practical experience through case studies and simulations, and network with consulting professionals.

Gaining practical experience in consulting or related fields through internships, co-op placements, or part-time positions can provide invaluable insights and exposure to the consulting industry. Internships, in particular, provide a unique opportunity to collaborate with experienced consultants, participate in client engagements, and gain hands-on experience in project management, data analysis, and client relationship management.

Consider using extracurricular activities, volunteer work, and leadership roles to develop and demonstrate your consulting-related skills and qualities. Whether you're leading a student organization, organizing community events, or competing in consulting-related competitions or case competitions, these experiences can help you showcase your leadership, teamwork, and problem-solving skills to potential consulting employers.

Do not underestimate the value of continuous learning and staying up-to-date on industry trends, emerging technologies, and consulting best practices. Subscribe to industry publications, blogs, and newsletters; attend conferences and networking events; and actively participate in online communities and forums to stay up-to-date on the latest developments in the consulting field. By demonstrating a commitment to lifelong learning and professional development, you will position yourself as a proactive and forward-thinking candidate in the competitive consulting field.

Gaining relevant experience

Getting relevant experience is an important step in starting a career as a consultant. While formal education gives a firm foundation of information and abilities, it is practical experience that truly distinguishes prospective consultants and prepares them for success in the profession. Aspiring consultants can get relevant experience through a variety of channels, each with its own set of learning, growth, and skill development possibilities.

Internships and co-op positions are among the most prevalent ways to get consulting experience. Many consulting businesses, as well as organizations in other sectors, have internship programs that allow students to gain hands-on experience working on real-world projects under the supervision of experienced consultants. Internships allow prospective consultants to use their academic knowledge in a practical situation, acquire important skills like problem solving and client communication, and receive firsthand experience with the day-to-day duties of consulting.

Part-time or freelance employment is another effective way to build consulting expertise. Many consultants begin their careers by providing their skills on a part-time or freelance basis, either individually or through platforms like Upwork and Freelancer. This enables aspiring consultants to obtain experience working with customers, managing projects, and delivering outcomes, all while developing a portfolio of work that displays their abilities to future companies or clients.

Volunteering may also be an effective way to obtain experience and make a difference while developing consulting skills. Many nonprofit, community, and humanitarian organizations rely on volunteers to assist with tasks such as strategy planning, program creation, and fundraising. Volunteering your time and talents allows you to obtain expertise in areas such as project management, stakeholder involvement, and problem solving, all of which are in great demand in the consulting profession.

Joining consulting-related student groups, clubs, or contests can give excellent chances for experience and skill development outside of the classroom. Many institutions offer student consulting clubs or case competition teams, which allow students to collaborate on consulting projects, solve real-world business challenges, and network with industry experts. Participating in these extracurricular activities will help you gain significant hands-on experience, expand your professional network, and demonstrate your enthusiasm and dedication to a career in consulting.

Informative interviews, mentorship, and networking are all valuable ways to get relevant experience and insights into the consulting sector. Reach out to people in consulting or similar sectors and ask if you may shadow them, interview them about their experiences, or get advice on how to start a consulting career. Building contacts with industry specialists may bring useful insights, chances for learning and advancement, and possible paths to internships, jobs, or freelance consulting work.

Creating Your Consulting Toolkit

Building your consulting toolbox entails gathering a varied and effective armory of skills, information, and resources that will enable you to face any problem and provide value to your customers. As you begin your career as a consultant, it is critical to develop a diverse range of tools and competencies that will enable you to thrive in the dynamic and fast-paced world of consulting.

First and foremost, improving your analytical abilities is essential for success in consulting. Consultants are frequently responsible for dissecting difficult issues, evaluating data, and drawing actionable conclusions to inform their suggestions and plans. Developing skills in data analysis, financial modeling, market research, and statistical analysis can help you obtain and understand information, recognize patterns and trends, and make educated judgments in consulting engagements.

Effective communication is another important skill in the consulting toolbox. As a consultant, you must present your ideas, insights, and suggestions to clients, stakeholders, and team members in a clear, convincing, and confident manner. Whether presenting findings to senior executives, facilitating workshops with frontline staff, or drafting reports for clients, strong verbal, written, and interpersonal communication skills are critical for developing rapport, fostering collaboration, and driving engagement in consulting projects.

Strategic thinking and problem-solving abilities are essential for success in consulting. Consultants frequently provide new solutions to complicated problems, overcome ambiguity and uncertainty, and generate positive change for their customers. Cultivating a strategic mentality, using critical thinking, and tackling challenges with creativity and pragmatism can help you uncover opportunities, overcome hurdles, and produce meaningful outcomes in consulting engagements.

Project management and organizational abilities are equally valuable elements in the consulting toolbox. Consultants must manage several projects, deadlines, and stakeholders at the same time, frequently in fast-paced, high-pressure circumstances. Developing skills in project management techniques, time management, and stakeholder involvement will allow you to effectively plan, execute, and deliver projects on schedule and under budget while also prioritizing quality and customer satisfaction.

Developing adaptability and resilience is critical for success in consulting. The consulting sector is characterized by fast change, increasing client demands, and altering market dynamics, all of which require consultants to negotiate uncertainty and ambiguity with confidence and composure. Developing the capacity to adapt to new surroundings, learn rapidly, and flourish in dynamic and demanding conditions will allow you to remain nimble and resilient in the face of change, preparing you for success in consulting engagements.

Establishing a strong professional network is an important tool in the consulting toolbox. Networking with industry professionals, mentors, peers, and clients may provide useful insights, chances for learning and improvement, and possible paths to internships, jobs, or freelance consulting contracts. Building and cultivating connections with people in the consulting profession will allow you to broaden your expertise, establish your reputation, and get access to vital resources and opportunities throughout your consulting career.

Developing your consulting toolkit entails acquiring a varied mix of skills, information, and resources that will enable you to thrive in the dynamic and competitive consulting environment. By honing your analytical skills, developing effective communication, strategic thinking, and problem-solving abilities, mastering project management and organizational skills, cultivating adaptability and resilience, and developing a strong professional network, you'll be well-prepared to take on any challenge and make a meaningful impact as a consultant.

Developing analytical and problem-solving skills.

Anyone interested in becoming a consultant should focus on developing analytical and problem-solving abilities. Consultants in the fast-paced and dynamic world of consulting continuously face challenging issues and must devise unique solutions to help customers achieve their objectives. Thus, improving these talents is critical for success in this competitive sector.

Let us begin by discussing analytical skills. Consultants must be able to evaluate huge volumes of data, derive useful insights, and generate meaningful findings to support their suggestions. This entails not just comprehending the data itself but also the context in which it is acquired and the ramifications for the client's operations. Developing skills in data analysis tools and techniques, such as statistical analysis, regression modeling, and data visualization, is critical for consultants who want to make informed decisions and deliver value to their customers.

Furthermore, problem-solving skills are at the heart of consulting. Companies often hire consultants to address complex business challenges like streamlining operations, formulating growth plans, or managing organizational change. Effective problem-solving entails breaking down complicated difficulties into manageable components, identifying core causes, and generating imaginative and practical solutions. Consultants must be able to think critically, approach challenges from several perspectives, and tailor their solutions to each client's specific requirements and objectives.

However, consultants must have great research abilities to obtain appropriate information and data to back up their suggestions. This entails undertaking extensive market research, industry analysis, and competition benchmarking to obtain insight into the client's business environment and identify opportunities and risks. Consultants must be skilled in synthesizing information from many sources, distinguishing truth from opinion, and communicating their conclusions to clients in a clear and persuasive manner.

In addition to technical abilities, consultants must develop soft skills, which are required for successful analytical and problem-solving. This includes good communication skills that allow you to clearly and persuasively explain complicated ideas and suggestions to customers and stakeholders. Consultants must also have great interpersonal skills in order to interact with team members, create connections with clients, and handle difficult circumstances with tact and diplomacy.

Consultants must always seek chances to improve their analytical and problem-solving abilities. This might include competing in case competitions, attending conferences and seminars, or studying advanced topics like data analytics, decision science, and problem-solving approaches. Consultants can also look for opportunities for real-world experience, such as internships, volunteer work, or part-time positions, to use their abilities in realistic situations and gain valuable insights into the consulting industry.

Anyone interested in becoming a consultant must first develop analytical and problem-solving abilities. Improving these talents, prospective consultants may set themselves apart in a competitive employment market, give useful insights and recommendations to their customers, and eventually make a significant contribution to the dynamic and gratifying world of consulting.

Communication and Presentation Skills.

Effective communication and presentation skills are essential for anyone pursuing a job as a consultant. In the fast-paced and dynamic world of consulting, consultants must continually communicate complex ideas, insights, and recommendations to clients, stakeholders, and team members in a clear, succinct, and compelling manner. As a result, improving these talents is critical to success and having a significant influence in the consulting sector.

Let us consider communication abilities. As a consultant, you must be able to effectively communicate your views and ideas, both orally and in writing. This includes not just expressing oneself clearly and simply but also adapting your communication style to the audience and circumstances. Strong verbal and written communication skills are critical for developing rapport, promoting cooperation, and driving engagement in consulting projects, whether you're presenting results to top executives, running workshops with front-line personnel, or producing client reports.

Successful communication in consulting requires active listening and empathy. Consultants must be able to listen intently to their clients' needs, worries, and goals while also demonstrating empathy and understanding in their interactions. This entails asking intelligent questions, requesting clarification as needed, and displaying genuine interest and concern for the client's viewpoint. Consultants may gain confidence and credibility from their clients by actively listening and displaying empathy, as well as ensuring that their recommendations are in line with the client's aims and priorities.

In addition to communication abilities, consultants must be able to effectively deliver their thoughts and suggestions to clients and stakeholders. This includes not just giving polished and professional presentations but also engaging with your audience and soliciting their involvement and input. Consultants must be able to organize their presentations clearly, use visual aids effectively, and convey their message confidently and enthusiastically. Consultants who produce visually appealing presentations may catch their audience's attention, effectively communicate their important points, and motivate action and buy-in from their customers.

Furthermore, consultants must be capable of conducting challenging talks and resolving disagreements successfully. Consulting engagements may be difficult due to stakeholder conflicts, resistance to change, or unforeseen impediments. Consultants must be able to handle these circumstances with tact and diplomacy, resolve issues constructively, and reach mutually accepted conclusions. Consultants who demonstrate strong conflict resolution and problem-solving abilities may gain client confidence and credibility and maintain healthy relationships throughout the consulting engagement.

Finally, consultants must actively seek chances to improve their communication and presentation abilities. This might include taking part in public speaking courses, attending communication training programs, or receiving feedback and coaching from mentors and coworkers. Consultants must also actively seek chances to practice and improve their abilities in real-world contexts, such as client presentations, team meetings, and networking events. Consultants may differentiate themselves in a competitive employment market, create strong client connections, and eventually thrive in the dynamic and exciting field of consulting by constantly refining their communication and presentation abilities.

Networking and Relationship Building

The development of a successful consulting profession requires networking and connection development. In the competitive and dynamic world of consulting, the ability to connect with others, form meaningful relationships, and use those relationships to further one's career is crucial.

Networking is more than just exchanging business cards or establishing contacts on social media; it is about developing meaningful relationships with people who can offer you support, direction, and chances throughout your career. Whether it's interacting with consulting professionals, alumni from your alma mater, or people in your target industries or sectors, networking allows you to exchange ideas, learn from others, and grow your professional network.

Industry gatherings, conferences, and networking mixers are among the most successful ways for consultants to network. These events allow you to meet and engage with experts from other sectors, share ideas and best practices, and form relationships with people who might become key contacts in the future. Attending these events helps you to not only broaden your network but also remain current on industry trends and advances.

Also, using online platforms like LinkedIn may be an effective technique for networking in the consulting profession. LinkedIn enables you to connect with people in your area, join industry-specific groups and communities, and participate in debates and information exchanges with peers and experts. Actively participating in online forums and communicating with people in your business, you may broaden your network, demonstrate your knowledge, and remain current on industry trends and possibilities.

Networking is more than simply connecting with people; it is also about giving back and helping your network. Giving back to your network, whether by mentoring junior professionals, offering advice and direction to peers, or making introductions and recommendations to individuals in your network, strengthens connections and fosters goodwill. By being a valued resource and helping others, you may build a strong and supportive network that will help you throughout your career.

Building relationships is also critical for success in consulting. To ensure project success, consultants must be able to establish and maintain excellent relationships with clients, stakeholders, and team members. This includes not only producing high-quality work but also successfully communicating, managing expectations, and establishing trust and rapport with coworkers.

Building excellent client connections is especially important in consulting, as delighted customers are more likely to give repeat business and referrals. Consultants must dedicate time and effort to knowing their customers' requirements, goals, and obstacles, and then adjust their strategy and communication style to fit those needs. By establishing trust, proving competence, and providing value to their customers, consultants may cultivate long-term partnerships that promote corporate success and growth.

Consultants must also establish excellent connections with stakeholders and team members to guarantee project success. This entails using good communication, cooperation, and conflict resolution to align goals and expectations, negotiate obstacles, and achieve consensus and alignment. By creating a good and collaborative team atmosphere, consultants may harness their team's overall experience and talents to create excellent results for their customers.

Networking and connection development are critical abilities for success in the consulting sector. Building real connections, and giving back to your network, you may broaden your professional network, get access to lucrative opportunities, and stay current on industry trends and changes. Furthermore, developing excellent connections with clients, stakeholders, and team members is critical for achieving effective project results and advancing your consulting career.

Develop your Consulting Brand

Creating your consulting brand is a critical step in establishing yourself as a credible and sought-after expert in the market. Your consulting brand is more than a logo or a slogan; it includes your unique value proposition, knowledge, reputation, and how people perceive you and your services. By proactively developing your consulting brand, you can set yourself apart from the competition, attract customers, and establish a successful consulting career.

Identifying your distinct value proposition is critical when developing your consulting brand. What differentiates you from other consultants? What special knowledge, skills, or insights do you bring to the table? Identifying your unique talents and capabilities enables you to establish yourself as an authority in your sector and express the value you provide to potential clients. Whether it's your extensive industry expertise, particular skill set, or innovative approach to problem solving, communicating your distinct value proposition is at the core of your consulting brand.

In today's digital world, having a good online presence is essential for growing your consulting brand. This involves developing a professional website that promotes your services, skills, and customer testimonials, as well as customizing your LinkedIn page to emphasize your professional experience and accomplishments. Also, actively participating in thought leadership activities such as authoring articles, attending industry forums, and speaking at conferences may help you position yourself as a reputable authority in your sector and boost your consultancy brand.

Developing a reputation for producing great results is critical to enhancing your consulting brand. Client testimonials, case studies, and success stories are effective ways to demonstrate your track record of accomplishment and establish trust with future clients. Consistently delivering high-quality work, exceeding client expectations, and generating positive word-of-mouth referrals, you can build your reputation and establish your consulting brand as synonymous with excellence and dependability.

Maintaining a strong professional network is essential for developing your consulting brand and growing your reach in the market. Networking with other consultants, industry professionals, and potential clients helps you to share ideas, work together on projects, and discover new prospects. Building great relationships within your network not only improves your consultancy brand, but it also opens the door to prospective partnerships, referrals, and collaborations that may help you elevate your brand and extend your clientele.

Having a consistent and unified brand identity across all touchpoints is critical for increasing brand awareness and generating trust with customers. This involves creating a professional brand image with a logo, color scheme, and visual components that reflect your business's personality and values. Consistency in message, tone of voice, and communication style across all media strengthens your consultancy brand and contributes to a strong and identifiable brand identity.

Define your niche and expertise.

Defining your area and expertise is an important step in establishing yourself as a consultant and pursuing a successful career in the field. Your niche is the specific sector or section of the market in which you specialize, whereas your expertise is the unique knowledge, skills, and experience that you bring to bear within that niche. By identifying your specialization and expertise, you may establish yourself as an authority in your sector, attract clients who require your specialized skills, and set yourself apart from the competition.

To begin, establish your specialty by restricting your attention to a single business, sector, or issue area in which you have extensive knowledge and skill. This might be based on your job experience, education, or personal preferences. For example, you may specialize in management consulting for the healthcare industry or offer financial consulting services to small firms.

By choosing a niche that corresponds to your interests and abilities, you may concentrate your efforts on building specialized knowledge and skills that are very useful to clients in that industry.

Once you've determined your specialty, the next step is to identify your competence within it. This entails recognizing your specific abilities, skills, and experiences that distinguish you from other consultants in the sector.

Consider your professional history, education, certifications, and any particular training or expertise you've gained over your work. What unique talents or information do you possess that are extremely beneficial to clients in your niche? This might be technical talents, industry-specific knowledge, problem-solving ability, or your own unique perspective.

Establishing yourself as an expert in your field necessitates continuous learning and development in order to stay current with industry trends, emerging technology, and best practices in your profession. This might include visiting industry conferences and seminars, obtaining further certifications or training programs, or participating in ongoing self-study to broaden your knowledge and skill set. By constantly learning and evolving in your industry, you can remain ahead of the competition and establish yourself as a valued adviser and thought leader.

Properly articulating your area and experience is critical for gaining customers and expanding your consulting firm. This includes clearly expressing your value proposition, target market, and distinguishing features in your marketing materials, website, and client contacts. By displaying your focus and experience, you can attract clients looking for specialized services while also demonstrating your reputation and authority in your sector.

Defining your area and expertise is a critical step in beginning a consulting career and establishing a successful consulting firm. By identifying a niche that aligns with your interests and expertise, defining your unique strengths and skills within that niche, constantly learning and developing within your field, and effectively communicating your niche and expertise to clients, you can position yourself as an expert in your field and attract clients who value your specialized services.

Creating a Personal Brand

Creating a personal brand is an effective way to distinguish yourself as a consultant and stand out in a competitive field. Your personal brand is more than a logo or a phrase; it represents your distinct beliefs, skills, expertise, and reputation. By developing a strong and authentic personal brand, you may attract customers, increase credibility, and set yourself apart from other consultants in the sector.

Creating a personal brand begins with understanding your unique value proposition. What differentiates you from other consultants? What particular talents, experiences, and characteristics do you bring to the table? Your value proposition should represent your distinct talents and expertise while communicating the value you provide to potential clients. Whether it's your extensive industry expertise, particular skill set, or creative approach to problem solving, communicating your value proposition is at the core of your personal brand.

Having a strong online presence is critical to developing your personal brand. This involves developing a professional website that promotes your services, skills, and customer testimonials, as well as customizing your LinkedIn page to emphasize your professional experience and accomplishments. Furthermore, actively participating in thought leadership activities such as authoring articles, attending industry forums, and speaking at conferences may help you position yourself as a trustworthy authority in your sector and raise your personal brand.

Developing a reputation for producing excellent outcomes is critical to enhancing your personal brand. Client testimonials, case studies, and success stories are effective ways to demonstrate your track record of accomplishment and establish trust with future clients. By consistently providing high-quality work, exceeding client expectations, and generating positive word-of-mouth referrals, you can build your reputation and establish your personal brand as synonymous with excellence and dependability.

Owning a consistent and unified brand identity across all touchpoints is critical for increasing brand awareness and generating trust with customers. This involves creating a professional brand image with a logo, color scheme, and visual components that reflect your business's personality and values. Consistency in messaging, tone of voice, and communication style across all media strengthens your personal brand and contributes to a strong and identifiable brand identity.

Creating an Online Presence.

Creating an online presence is critical for any consultant trying to develop and prosper in today's digital landscape. In a day where the internet is the major source of information and communication, having a strong online presence is critical for reaching out to new clients, demonstrating your knowledge, and establishing a reputation in your sector.

Creating a decent website is an important step in developing your online presence. Your website serves as your digital shop and is often the first point of contact for potential customers. It should be well-designed, simple to use, and provide pertinent information about your services, skills, and contact information. Your website should also feature a portfolio of your work, customer testimonials, and case studies to show off your expertise and track record of accomplishment.

In addition to your website, using social media platforms is an efficient way to increase your online visibility as a consultant. Platforms such as LinkedIn, Twitter, and Facebook enable you to connect with professionals in your sector, exchange useful ideas and material, and interact with your audience. LinkedIn, in particular, is a valuable resource for consultants since it allows you to demonstrate your professional expertise, connect with new customers and colleagues, and join industry-specific groups and communities.

Generating and distributing great content is critical for growing your online presence and establishing yourself as an authority in your sector. This may involve publishing blog posts, essays, or whitepapers about issues important to your area, sharing insights and best practices on social media, or producing films or podcasts to demonstrate your knowledge. By continuously producing and distributing quality content, you may attract and engage your target audience, demonstrate your knowledge and experience, and establish authority in your sector.

Regularly participating in online groups and forums relevant to your field might help you establish an online profile as a consultant. Participating in debates, answering questions, and offering helpful insights may all help you establish yourself as a competent and trustworthy expert in your subject. Furthermore, attending online events, webinars, and virtual conferences allows you to interact with industry people, exchange knowledge, and broaden your network. Optimizing your web presence for search engines is critical for improving exposure and acquiring new customers. This includes using relevant keywords to improve your website, developing high-quality, search engine-optimized content, and establishing backlinks from trustworthy websites in your field. Optimizing your online presence for search engines can help you rank higher in search results and attract more organic visitors to your website.

Finding Your First Client

Your first clients is an important milestone for anybody starting out as a consultant. It represents the start of your consulting career, when you will be able to apply your knowledge, make a concrete effect, and establish yourself as a trusted adviser in your industry. Finding your first clients may be intimidating, but it is a doable and attainable objective with the appropriate technique and mentality.

Use your current network and relationships to locate new clients. Contact old coworkers, classmates, mentors, and friends who may require your consulting skills or may refer you to potential customers. Personal referrals and word-of-mouth recommendations are frequently the most successful strategies to obtain your initial clients since they come with an inherent degree of trust and trustworthiness.

Attend industry events, conferences, and networking mixers to build your professional network and meet new clients. These events give you an excellent opportunity to meet decision-makers and influencers in your target market, learn about industry trends and issues, and demonstrate your knowledge and value proposition. Be proactive in introducing yourself, starting discussions, and exchanging contact information with people who could be interested in your consulting services.

Additionally, use internet platforms and social media to market your consulting services and attract new clients. Create a professional LinkedIn profile that shows your experience, knowledge, and services, and actively participate with your network by offering useful ideas, taking part in discussions, and connecting with possible clients. Consider building a professional website or blog to promote your experience, publish case studies and testimonials, and provide helpful tools and material to potential clients.

Try providing your consulting services for free or at a reduced charge to gather experience, expand your portfolio, and create a reputation in your sector. Nonprofits, startups, and small enterprises sometimes have limited resources, but they may be eager to collaborate with consultants who may offer significant experience and direction. Offering your skills at discounted charge or pro-bono allows you to gain important experience, create client connections, and generate favorable word-of-mouth recommendations that can lead to future paid possibilities.

When searching for your initial clientele, be aggressive and persistent in your outreach efforts. Follow up with potential leads, offer unique proposals or pitches that show you understand their needs and how you can assist them in solving their challenges, and communicate in a timely and professional manner. Building relationships with potential clients takes time and effort, so be patient and persistent in your quest to find your first clients.

Acquiring your first clients is a vital step in establishing a career as a consultant. You can successfully secure your first clients and start your consulting career by leveraging your existing network, attending industry events, utilizing online platforms, offering your services pro bono or at a discounted rate, and being proactive and persistent in your outreach efforts. Remember to approach each potential client with professionalism, passion, and a real desire to offer value and make a good impact, and you'll be well on your way to establishing a profitable consultancy.

Leveraging Your Network

Starting a consulting profession requires using your network. Your network is a valuable resource that may assist you in managing consulting problems and possibilities. Utilizing your network can assist in creating opportunities and establishing yourself as a reputable expert within your field, whether you are at the beginning stages or aiming to broaden your influence.

One of the first stages of using your network is to identify your current contacts and determine how they might help you advance your consulting career. This includes contacting previous coworkers, classmates, mentors, and acquaintances who may be able to give useful information, introductions, or possibilities. Personal ties are frequently the cornerstone of effective networking, so don't be afraid to reconnect with people who may help you on your consulting path.

Attending industry events, conferences, and networking mixers is an excellent method to broaden your professional network and meet possible clients, collaborators, and mentors. These events give an excellent opportunity to meet decision-makers, learn about industry trends and advances, and demonstrate your knowledge and value proposition. Be proactive in introducing yourself, starting discussions, and exchanging contact information with people who could be interested in your consulting services.

Furthermore, using online platforms and social media is an effective way to broaden your network and engage with possible clients and partners. Platforms such as LinkedIn allow you to exhibit your experience, knowledge, and services while also connecting with experts in your sector. Actively connect with your network by offering useful ideas, participating in discussions, and contacting new clients and partners who could be interested in your services.

Consider joining industry-specific clubs and communities, both online and offline, to broaden your network and meet like-minded people. These organizations give excellent chances to exchange ideas, share best practices, and work on projects with others who have similar interests and aims. By actively participating in these forums, you may make significant contacts and position yourself as an important member of your industry.

Don't underestimate the value of referrals and recommendations from your network in acquiring new clients and prospects. Personal referrals from trustworthy contacts are frequently the most efficient technique to gain new clients and establish a reputation in your industry. Be proactive in seeking recommendations from pleased clients, mentors, and coworkers who can attest to your experience and services. Also, if feasible, reciprocate by providing references and recommendations to people in your network.

Finally, using your network is an effective technique for developing a successful consulting profession. By broaden your reach, acquire clients, and position yourself as a trusted advisor in your profession by exploiting internet platforms, participating in industry-specific forums, and nurturing referrals and recommendations. Remember to approach networking with sincerity, professionalism, and a real desire to offer value to your contacts, and you'll be well on your way to using your network to succeed in your consulting career.

Market and promote your services.

Marketing and advertising are the life wire of any business or services. Marketing and Promotion of your services are critical components of establishing a successful consulting profession. As a consultant, you have unique skills and insights to offer; nevertheless, without strong marketing and promotion, it can be difficult to attract customers and demonstrate your value proposition. As a result, creating a deliberate strategy for marketing and advertising your services is critical for establishing yourself as a reliable adviser and attracting clients who can benefit from your experience.

One of the first steps in marketing and advertising your services is to define a clear target market and ideal clientele. Understanding your potential clientele, including their goals, difficulties, and pain spots, is critical for developing focused marketing messages and adapting your services to their unique requirements. By identifying your target market, you can tailor your marketing efforts to reach and attract potential consumers who are most likely to benefit from your offerings.

Once you've identified your target market, create a compelling value proposition that clearly illustrates the distinct benefits and advantages of working with you as a consultant. Your value proposition should clearly communicate the problem you address, the results you achieve, and the distinct value you provide to clients. By properly defining your value proposition, you can set yourself apart from rivals and attract clients looking for the specialized knowledge and solutions you provide.

Creating a strong web presence is vital for selling and promoting your consulting services. This involves developing a professional website that promotes your services, skills, and customer testimonials, as well as customizing your LinkedIn page to emphasize your professional experience and accomplishments. Furthermore, actively participating in thought leadership activities such as authoring articles, attending industry forums, and presenting at conferences may help you position yourself as a recognized authority in your subject, increasing your exposure and credibility.

Developing a content marketing plan may be an efficient technique to acquire new clients and demonstrate your competence. This entails developing and distributing quality information such as blog posts, essays, whitepapers, or films that address your target market's requirements, issues, and pain points. By providing unique insights and solutions in your content, you can position yourself as a trustworthy adviser and attract clients looking for your experience and counsel. Networking and developing contacts with potential customers and industry leaders is an effective way to sell and promote your consulting services. Attending business events, conferences, and networking mixers is an excellent way to meet decision-makers, learn about industry trends and advances, and demonstrate your knowledge and value proposition. By actively participating in these events and interacting with potential customers and collaborators, you can form important relationships and position yourself as a trustworthy advisor in your area.

Also, providing free consultations or workshops is an efficient way to demonstrate your competence and attract new clients. By delivering value upfront and displaying your knowledge and skills, you may gain potential clients' confidence and credibility while positioning yourself as a viable resource for their requirements. Furthermore, giving special offers or discounts to new consumers might help entice those who are hesitant to commit to your services at first.

In a nut shell, marketing and promoting your services as a consultant necessitate a strategic approach that includes defining your target market, developing a compelling value proposition, establishing a strong online presence, creating valuable content, networking and building relationships, and providing free consultations or workshops. By successfully adopting these tactics, you may attract customers, demonstrate your knowledge, and establish a lucrative and influential consulting firm.

Pitch and Proposals

In any business Pitching and proposals must be taken seriously, they are the key components of launching a successful consulting career. As a consultant, your ability to successfully present your services and create attractive proposals might be the difference between landing and losing customers. A well-executed pitch and proposal not only illustrate your knowledge and talents but also your grasp of the client's requirements and how you can add value to their firm.

When creating your pitch, be sure to personalize it to the client's unique wants and issues. Take the time to investigate the client's industry, rivals, and pain points, and then determine how your services may meet their unique needs and bring value to their firm. Displaying a thorough awareness of the client's needs and concerns, you may establish yourself as a reliable adviser capable of providing unique solutions to their problems.

Creating a persuasive proposal requires explicitly outlining the scope of work, deliverables, timetable, and price for your services. Your proposal should include the exact services you will offer, the techniques you will employ to achieve results, and the expected outcomes for the client. To distinguish yourself from the competition and illustrate why you are the best option for the customer, emphasize your unique value offer, knowledge, and track record of success.

As said earlier, when pitching and presenting your proposal to the customer, it is critical to emphasize the benefits and value of your services rather than merely their characteristics. Clearly convey how your services will assist the customer in achieving their goals, resolving challenges, and driving meaningful outcomes for their business. By emphasizing the benefits and worth of your services, you may attract the client's attention and persuade them of the value you can bring to their firm.

Excellent communication and storytelling are essential components of a successful presentation and proposal. Use captivating tales, case studies, and customer testimonials to demonstrate how your services have helped other clients overcome similar obstacles and achieve their objectives. Sharing real-world examples and success stories will help you create credibility and trust with the customer, making your presentation more powerful and appealing.

Also, be prepared to answer any questions or concerns that the customer may have during the pitch and proposal process. Anticipate potential objections and be prepared to provide meaningful solutions that address the client's concerns while reassuring them of your ability to deliver results. You can boost your chances of earning the client's business by exhibiting your experience and confidence in dealing with their problems.

Pitching and proposals are vital skills for beginning a successful consulting career. You can increase your chances of winning clients and building a successful consulting practice by tailoring your pitch to the client's specific needs, creating a compelling proposal that clearly outlines the scope of work and value of your services, emphasizing the benefits and value of your services, effectively communicating your expertise through storytelling and case studies, and addressing any client concerns or objections.

Providing Exceptional Consulting Services.

Delivering outstanding consulting services is essential to a successful consulting profession. Your customers rely on you as a consultant for experience, direction, and recommendations to help them overcome obstacles, achieve their objectives, and create organizational success. As a result, it's critical to approach your business with professionalism, focus, and a desire to provide value to your clients.

The first stages of providing outstanding consulting services is to set clear goals and expectations for your customers. Before commencing any project, take the time to grasp the client's goals, priorities, and expected outcomes. Collaborate with the client to create precise project goals, milestones, and deliverables, and ensure that both sides have clear expectations for the engagement. Setting clear goals and expectations ahead of time can help ensure a successful and productive consulting session.

Efficient communication is critical to providing excellent consulting services. Maintain open and honest contact with your clients throughout the project, offering regular updates on progress, addressing any issues or problems that may occur, and soliciting feedback on your efforts. Actively listen to your clients' wants and concerns, and be attentive and available to resolve any questions or difficulties that may arise. Maintaining excellent communication, you can establish a strong and collaborative connection with your clients, ensuring that their requirements are addressed and expectations are surpassed throughout the engagement.

Providing outstanding consulting services necessitates a thorough awareness of your client's sector, business, and difficulties. Take the time to study and become acquainted with the client's industry environment, competitive landscape, and market trends, then use your experience to deliver important insights and suggestions customized to their unique requirements. By demonstrating a thorough understanding of the client's business and industry, you can establish yourself as a trusted adviser capable of providing helpful counsel and solutions to help them reach their goals.

In addition, focus on providing concrete outcomes and value to your clientele. Your customers employ you as a consultant to help them solve issues, achieve goals, and create organizational success. As a result, it is critical to focus on generating quantifiable outcomes and real results that reflect the impact of your efforts. Track and measure project progress against key performance indicators and success measures, and give frequent updates to customers on the findings. By concentrating on providing concrete value and outcomes, you can gain your clients' confidence and credibility while also ensuring that they recognize the value of your services.

Providing outstanding consulting services necessitates a commitment to ongoing learning and progress. Stay up-to-date on industry trends, best practices, and emerging technology in your profession, and look for new ways to broaden your knowledge and skill set. Invest in professional development options like training programs, certificates, and workshops to improve your skills and remain ahead of the competition. By constantly learning and developing, you can offer your clients new solutions and experienced advice that will help their businesses succeed.

Develop good ties with your clients is critical for providing excellent consulting services. Take the time to learn your clients' specific wants, preferences, and communication styles, and then customize your approach appropriately. Proactively anticipate their needs and provide proactive solutions and ideas that align with their goals and objectives. By building trust, rapport, and a solid working relationship with your clients, you can promote a collaborative and productive collaboration that results in effective solutions.

Maintaining a high degree of professionalism and honesty is critical to providing excellent consulting services. Always maintain honesty, openness, and integrity in all dealings with clients, coworkers, and stakeholders. Adhere to your field's ethical standards and best practices, and put your clients' best interests first. By exhibiting professionalism and integrity in your job, you may gain credibility, trust, and confidence from your clients, ensuring that they have a pleasant working experience with you.

Furthermore, providing outstanding consulting services frequently necessitates the capacity to adjust and pivot in response to shifting circumstances and changing client demands. Be adaptable and nimble in your approach, and be prepared to change your tactics and recommendations as needed to accommodate new difficulties or opportunities. Maintain a proactive approach to spotting possible hazards and possibilities, and be ready to provide creative and inventive solutions that suit your clients' evolving demands. Demonstrating flexibility and adaptability in your approach, you can successfully negotiate complex and dynamic consulting engagements and provide excellent results for your customers.

Establishing Client Relationships.

Establishing client contacts is an essential component of beginning a career as a consultant. Building strong and pleasant connections with your clients is critical not just for obtaining business but also for ensuring long-term success and happiness for all parties involved. The success of your client relationships as a consultant depends on your ability to create rapport, communicate effectively, understand your customers' needs, and produce results.

First and foremost, creating trust is essential for developing successful client connections. Trust is the foundation of every successful collaboration, and clients must be certain that you have their best interests at heart and have the experience and ability to produce results. Building trust and credibility requires you to demonstrate integrity, honesty, and reliability in all of your dealings with clients. To win your clients' trust and confidence, be open about your skills, set realistic expectations, and keep your promises.

Establishing customer connections also requires effective communication. Clear and honest communication is critical for ensuring that all sides agree on goals, expectations, and outcomes. Take the time to actively listen to your clients' requirements and problems and convey your thoughts, recommendations, and progress updates in an understandable and succinct manner. Be responsive and accessible to your clients, and take proactive steps to resolve any questions or concerns that may emerge. You may create a great connection and understanding with your clients and meet their demands throughout the relationship by encouraging open and honest communication.

Understanding your clients' requirements and goals is critical to building effective client relationships. Take the time to conduct extensive discovery sessions and ask probing questions to better understand your clients' objectives, difficulties, and priorities. Pay close attention to their replies and ask for clarification as needed to ensure that you have a clear knowledge of their requirements and expectations. By displaying a genuine interest in knowing your clients' wants and goals, you can personalize your solutions and recommendations to match their individual demands and give them maximum value.

In addition to knowing your clients' requirements, you should display empathy and emotional intelligence in your interactions with them. Recognize that each customer is unique and may have varying opinions, preferences, and communication styles. Adapt your approach as needed, and be attentive to your clients' emotions and worries. Demonstrate empathy and compassion, and take a proactive approach to any obstacles or concerns that occur. By displaying empathy and emotional intelligence, you may establish a great connection and trust with your clients, fostering pleasant and productive partnerships.

Achieving outcomes and offering value are critical for building strong client connections. Finally, clients employ consultants to help them solve issues, achieve goals, and drive organizational success. As a result, you must prioritize providing actual outcomes and contributing value to your clients' organizations. Be proactive in finding areas for development and innovation, and offer unique and effective solutions that meet your clients' demands and goals. By consistently providing results and offering value, you can demonstrate your knowledge and commitment to your clients' success while also establishing long-term and mutually beneficial partnerships.

Creating and Having a client contacts is a critical component of beginning a career as a consultant. Building trust, fostering open and transparent communication, understanding your clients' needs and objectives, demonstrating empathy and emotional intelligence, delivering results, and adding value can all help you establish strong and successful client relationships that will contribute to your long-term success as a consultant.

Managing Projects Effectively

Effective project management is a key ability for every consultant who wants to start a successful career in the industry. As a consultant, you will most likely be in charge of managing a variety of projects, ranging from small-scale initiatives to large-scale implementations, and your ability to manage these projects quickly and effectively will have a big impact on both your own and your clients' success.

One of the first stages of efficient project management is to define clear project objectives and deliverables. Before you begin any project, work with your customer to identify its scope, goals, and objectives. Before you begin any project, work with your customer to identify its scope, goals, and objectives. Establishing defined project objectives and deliverables beforehand ensures that everyone involved understands the project's purpose and expectations.

Successful project management necessitates meticulous planning and organization. Create a thorough project plan that describes the project's tasks, milestones, and deadlines, and then assign resources and duties accordingly. When creating the project plan, keep budget, timing, and resource availability in mind, and be ready to alter and adapt as needed during the project's lifespan. With a well-defined project plan in place, you can guarantee that the project stays on track and moves toward its goals in a timely and effective manner.

Communication is required for successful project management. Maintain open and transparent communication with your team members, clients, and stakeholders throughout the project's lifespan. Provide frequent status reports on project progress, address emerging concerns or issues, and gather feedback from stakeholders to meet their requirements and expectations. By encouraging clear and open communication, you can develop trust and collaboration among project stakeholders, ensuring that everyone is working toward the same objective.

In addition to communication, good project management necessitates strong leadership and decision-making abilities. As the project manager, you will be in charge of leading the project team, making crucial decisions, and resolving any difficulties or disputes that emerge. Be proactive in identifying and resolving possible risks and problems, and be prepared to make harsh decisions when required to keep the project on schedule. By exhibiting great leadership and decision-making abilities, you may inspire confidence and trust in your team and guarantee that the project accomplishes its objectives.

Moreover, good project management requires monitoring and supervising project progress to ensure that it continues on schedule and within budget. Regularly assess project milestones, timeframes, and budgets, identifying and resolving any deviations or anomalies. Take proactive steps to resolve any difficulties or delays that arise, and be prepared to change the project plan as needed to keep the project on track. Continuous monitoring and regulation of project progress can eliminate risks and ensure successful and timely project completion.

Good project management entails using relevant technologies and processes to optimize project workflows and enhance efficiency. Depending on the nature and complexity of the project, you may need to apply project management tools, such as Asana, Trello, or Microsoft Project, to plan tasks, track progress, and engage with team members. These tools may help you stay organized, keep track of deadlines, and ensure that everyone is on the same page throughout the project.

Furthermore, good project management involves a proactive approach to risk management. Identify any risks and uncertainties that might affect the project's success, and establish ways to manage or address them proactively. This may entail completing risk assessments, making contingency plans, and allocating resources to handle possible hazards effectively. By predicting and managing possible risks early on, you can minimize their influence on the project and guarantee that it continues on schedule.

Moreover, good project management entails developing a collaborative and cohesive team atmosphere. It's critical to build a healthy and supportive team culture where team members feel respected, empowered, and driven to deliver their best work as the project manager. Encourage open communication, cooperation, and knowledge-sharing among team members, and give chances for professional growth and development. By building a collaborative and cohesive team atmosphere, you can maximize team performance and guarantee that everyone is working towards the same objective.

In addition to managing internal project teams, successful project management also requires managing client expectations and relationships. Keep your clients informed and involved throughout the project lifecycle, offering frequent updates on progress, resolving any issues or questions they may have, and requesting input on their satisfaction with the project. By actively managing client expectations and relationships, you can guarantee that your clients are pleased with the project outcomes and preserve strong, long-term connections with them.

However, good project management involves a commitment to ongoing development and learning. Reflect on each project's accomplishments and problems, and suggest opportunities for development and growth. Seek input from team members, clients, and stakeholders, and utilize this feedback to develop your project management methods and practices. Additionally, engage in continual professional development and training to stay current on the newest project management approaches, technologies, and best practices. Consistently upgrading your project management abilities and expertise, you can guarantee that you'll be able to face new problems and achieve great outcomes in your consulting career.

Handling Challenges and Difficult Clients

Navigating obstacles and dealing with difficult customers are unavoidable components of starting a career as a consultant. While consulting may be beneficial, it also comes with its fair share of hurdles and complications. Handling these problems properly is vital for sustaining great client relationships and attaining success in your consulting profession.

It's necessary to address difficulties from a proactive and solution-oriented perspective. Rather than perceiving obstacles as impediments, perceive them as opportunities for development and learning. Accept obstacles as a chance to show off your problem-solving abilities and resilience, and approach them with a positive attitude and a desire to discover innovative solutions.

Excellent communication is key in resolving issues. It is critical when dealing with obstacles and difficult clients. Maintain open and honest contact with your clients, and handle any concerns or issues that occur swiftly and professionally. Listen intently to your clients' suggestions and concerns, and seek to grasp their perspective and requirements.

It's important to create limits and manage expectations with a tough clientele. Establish clear expectations for the scope of work, deliverables, timeframes, and communication routes at the beginning of the engagement, ensuring agreement from all parties. Be strong but polite in enforcing limits, and express any modifications or departures from the initial agreement quickly and clearly.

Dealing with tough consumers requires patience and understanding. Understand that clients may be suffering from their own issues and stresses, and approach encounters with empathy and compassion. Listen intently to their worries, acknowledge their feelings, and display understanding and compassion in your replies. Demonstrating patience and empathy, you can establish rapport and trust with tough clients and foster a more pleasant and productive working relationship.

Moreover, it's crucial to stay professional and collected when presented with problems or unpleasant situations. Avoid responding hastily or emotionally, and instead, reply calmly and sensibly to any concerns or disagreements that emerge. Maintain a professional approach at all times, especially in stressful situations, and endeavor to identify mutually beneficial solutions that meet the client's concerns while also safeguarding your own interests and limits. In addition, seek help and direction from mentors, coworkers, or industry peers. Consult with trustworthy experts who have experience handling similar situations, and seek their thoughts and guidance on how to address the unique issues you're facing. By leveraging the assistance and experience of others, you may learn useful views and techniques for solving issues and managing challenging customers more successfully.

Scaling Your Consulting Business

Scaling your consulting firm is an important step toward boosting your career and long-term success as a consultant. It entails strategically extending your operations, boosting your customer base, and raising your income while preserving the quality of your services. Scaling your consulting firm takes meticulous strategy, execution, and a dedication to ongoing improvement. Here are some important tactics to consider while expanding your consulting business:

1. **Utilize Your Expertise:** As a consultant, your expertise and knowledge are your most important assets. To expand your consulting firm, specialize in a particular area where you have a distinct skill set or domain knowledge. Concentrate on areas where you can deliver great value to your customers and set yourself apart from the competition.

2. **Create a Strong Brand:** Developing a strong brand identity is critical for growing your consulting firm. Invest in branding efforts to establish a professional and appealing brand image that resonates with your target audience. Create a consistent brand statement, logo, and visual identity that communicates your value proposition and distinguishes you in the market.

3. **Expand Your Service Offerings:** To grow your consulting firm, try broadening your service offerings to meet your clients' changing demands. Identify additional services or solutions that complement your expertise and provide value to your clients. Diversifying your service offerings allows you to acquire new clients while increasing revenue streams.

4. **Form Strategic Partnerships:** Collaborating with other individuals or organizations can help you grow your consulting firm. Collaborate with complementary service providers, industry associations, or networking groups to broaden your reach and get access to new clients. Strategic alliances can also provide essential resources, experience, and assistance as you expand your firm.

5. **Implement Scalable Systems and Processes:** Streamlining your operations and developing scalable systems and processes are critical for growing your consulting firm. Invest in technology and automation solutions to improve administrative efficiency, project management, and client communication. Standardizing and improving your procedures will boost efficiency, productivity, and scalability.

6. **Focus on Client Retention and Satisfaction:** While recruiting new clients is critical for growing your consulting firm, maintaining existing ones is just as important. To promote client loyalty and long-term relationships, focus on providing outstanding service and value. Invest in customer satisfaction efforts like feedback surveys, regular check-ins, and customized service to keep your clients happy and keen to engage with you.

7. **Hire and Develop Talent:** As your consulting firm expands, you should consider recruiting more people to help with your increasing operations. Invest in recruiting, training, and developing skilled workers who share your values and can help your organization thrive. Building a solid team of qualified specialists allows you to increase your capacity, take on greater projects, and service more clients.

8. **Invest in Marketing and Firm Development:** In order to attract new customers and prospects, your consulting firm must engage in proactive marketing and business development. Create a complete marketing plan that combines both online and offline techniques to boost your exposure and reach your intended audience. Invest in networking, content marketing, social media, and other

promotional initiatives to create leads and grow your clientele.

9. **Assess and change:** Finally, to guarantee the effective expansion of your consulting firm, you need to regularly assess your progress and change your strategy as needed. Regularly evaluate key performance metrics, customer input, market trends, and the competitive environment to find areas for improvement and change. Staying adaptable and sensitive to market developments allows you to efficiently build your consulting firm and achieve long-term growth.

Hiring Support Staff

Starting a career as a consultant may be hectic, you may find that your workload increases and you need more assistance managing your expanding firm. Hiring support workers may be a strategic decision that allows you to streamline processes, enhance productivity, and focus on high-value tasks that drive business growth. However, employing the correct support personnel takes considerable research and preparation to ensure that they connect with your company's goals and contribute positively to its success.

When employing support workers for your consulting firm, it is critical to clearly outline the tasks and responsibilities you want them to do. Examine your present workload and identify particular activities or locations where further assistance is required. Having a comprehensive idea of the jobs you need to fill, whether they are administrative, client communication, project management, or other operational duties, can assist you in identifying the abilities and attributes that potential candidates must possess.

Once you've determined the jobs you need to fill, identify the required abilities and traits in support workers. Consider appropriate experience, technical capabilities, communication ability, organizational skills, and a cultural fit with your company. Look for people who have the ideal blend of talents and attributes that connect with your company's values and provide value to your team dynamics.

During the process of hiring support workers for your consulting firm, consider using several recruitment channels to reach a varied pool of prospects. This may involve advertising job openings on internet job boards, utilizing professional networking platforms, contacting industry groups or organizations, and requesting references from colleagues or peers. Casting a wide net and using numerous recruiting channels, you may improve your chances of finding competent applicants who meet your specific hiring requirements.

During the interview process, evaluate individuals' talents, experience, and cultural fit with your organization. Ask probing questions to learn about their previous experiences, problem-solving skills, and alignment with your company's beliefs. Consider conducting practical exams or exercises to assess candidates' technical abilities and ability to complete the required tasks efficiently. Conducting extensive interviews and evaluations, you can ensure that you are hiring support personnel who are a good fit for your consulting firm.

Once you've found acceptable individuals, it's critical to efficiently onboard and educate them to ensure their success in their new jobs. Provide clear direction on their tasks, expectations, and performance goals, as well as extensive training to provide them with the skills and information they need to succeed in their roles. Create a helpful and inclusive work atmosphere in which support personnel feel respected, empowered, and inspired to do their best.

As your consulting firm grows and evolves, evaluate your workforce requirements on a regular basis and make changes as needed to meet your business objectives. Be proactive in altering your employment plan to match your company's evolving demands, whether that means adding more support workers, reallocating tasks, or reorganizing jobs. By constantly analyzing and adjusting your staffing strategy, you can ensure that you have the necessary support personnel in place to fuel the success and development of your consulting firm.

It is critical to create a collaborative and inclusive work environment that values cooperation and mutual respect. Encourage open communication and cooperation among team members, and provide support personnel with the opportunity to contribute their thoughts and opinions to the company's overall success. Fostering a healthy and inclusive work culture may help your support personnel develop a strong sense of camaraderie and collaboration, resulting in higher morale, productivity, and job satisfaction.

Consider providing competitive remuneration and benefits packages to recruit and retain top personnel for your support staff roles. Conduct market research to learn about the industry norms for remuneration and benefits in your region, and make sure your offerings are competitive enough to attract eligible individuals. When building your compensation and benefits packages, consider income, health benefits, retirement plans, professional development opportunities, and work-life balance programs. Competitive wages and benefits enable you to recruit and retain exceptional support workers dedicated to your consulting firm's success.

As your consulting firm expands, consider creating performance management tools to review and acknowledge the efforts of your support team. Establish clear performance standards and goals for support staff jobs, and give frequent feedback and coaching to help them meet their objectives. Recognize and reward top performers for their contributions to the company, whether with monetary bonuses, promotions, or other incentives. Implementing performance management systems will motivate and engage your support workers, leading to improved performance and outcomes for your consulting firm.

In addition to recruiting support people inside, think about outsourcing specific activities or services to external vendors or contractors to supplement your expertise and resources. Outsourcing may be a cost-effective and adaptable method for handling specialized activities or projects that need unique skills or resources.

To guarantee a successful partnership, thoroughly examine potential vendors or contractors and set clear expectations and agreements when outsourcing administrative chores, IT support, marketing efforts, or other responsibilities. Strategic outsourcing allows you to get access to specialized expertise and resources while keeping your own resources focused on key business operations and strategic goals.

Recruiting support people is an important step toward growing your consulting firm and attaining long-term success. You can build a strong team of support staff by carefully defining roles and responsibilities, identifying desired skills and qualities, fostering a collaborative and inclusive work environment, offering competitive compensation and benefits, implementing performance management processes, and considering outsourcing opportunities. With the correct support team in place, you can efficiently manage your workload, simplify operations, and focus on providing value to your customers, resulting in the success of your consulting business.

Expanding your service offerings

As you begin your career as a consultant, broadening your service offerings is an important step in establishing yourself as a diverse and valued resource for your customers. While you may initially focus on a single specialization or area of expertise, broadening your service offerings may lead to new prospects, a broader range of clients, and more revenue streams. Expanding your service offerings necessitates a careful assessment of your abilities, knowledge, and market needs, as well as a systematic approach to discovering and developing new service offerings that correspond with your company's objectives and customer demands.

One strategy to diversify your service options is to increase your knowledge of your current specialty. As a consultant, you are most likely to have specialized knowledge and abilities in a specific sector or topic area. Consider broadening your skills by learning more in relevant fields or providing more services that complement your current ones. For example, if you specialize in marketing advice, you may broaden your offering to include social media management, content marketing, and digital advertising. Expanding on your current knowledge, you may deliver more complete solutions to your clients and set yourself apart from the competition.

Consider expanding your service offerings to include new sectors or markets. While you may have experience in one field, looking into prospects in neighboring industries or new markets might help you expand your customer base and income potential. Conduct market research to identify sectors or markets with unmet needs or development potential, and consider how your skills and knowledge can help in these areas. For example, if you specialize in healthcare consulting, you may look for possibilities in technology or finance that would benefit from your knowledge of healthcare rules and processes. Expanding into new sectors or marketplaces allows you to reach new clients and diversify your revenue streams.

Providing specialized or specialty services that address specific pain areas or issues for your clientele. Identify areas with a high need for specialist skills or services, and create offers to meet those demands. For example, if you specialize in project management consulting, you may provide specialized services like risk management consulting, change management consulting, and agile project management training. Offering specialized services allows you to attract clients looking for bespoke solutions to their specific difficulties while also positioning yourself as an authority in your sector.

Using technology and innovation to broaden your service offerings would help to attract new customers. Accept new technology, techniques, and processes that can improve your consulting services and allow you to provide more value to your clients. For example, you may provide virtual consulting services, online training programs, or tailored software solutions that use artificial intelligence or data analytics to tackle complicated challenges. Embracing technology and innovation, you can broaden your service offerings beyond traditional consulting services and satisfy your clients' increasing demands in the digital era.

Scaling your operations

Scaling your operations is critical to establishing a successful consulting career. As your consulting firm expands, you'll need to adapt and extend your operations to meet rising demand, handle larger projects, and efficiently serve an expanding client base. Scaling your operations includes improving your company processes, utilizing technology and automation, assembling a strong workforce, and implementing scalable systems to support your growth and long-term success.

One critical component of growing your operations is refining your business processes to increase efficiency and productivity. Examine your present workflows to discover places where you may optimize procedures, eliminate bottlenecks, and cut inefficiencies. This might include standardizing procedures, following best practices, and using technology to automate repetitive operations. By streamlining your business processes, you may increase productivity, reduce mistakes, and provide better results to your clients.

Efficient operational scaling necessitates the use of technology and automation. Invest in technological tools and software solutions that help automate regular operations, simplify project management, and enhance team communication and cooperation. This might include project management software, CRM systems, communication tools, and collaboration platforms. By leveraging technology and automation, you may improve productivity, minimize manual effort, and grow your operations more successfully.

Another important aspect of growing your consulting business is assembling a solid team of professionals. As your company expands, you will need to recruit more employees to support your increasing operations and serve your growing clientele. Ensure that exceptional experts who share your values, possess the necessary skills and knowledge, and are committed to delivering high-quality service to your clients are hired. Invest in training and development initiatives to help your team members advance and flourish in their positions. By assembling a great workforce, you can grow your operations and provide excellent outcomes to your customers.

Creating a scalable systems and procedures is critical for controlling growth and maintaining consistency as your operations expand. Create standardized protocols and procedures for project management, client communication, and other critical areas of your business operations. Make sure these systems are flexible and responsive to your company's changing needs and development. Implementing scalable systems and procedures can help you ensure consistency, quality, and efficiency throughout your operations as they grow and develop.

Furthermore, as your activities grow, you must monitor and measure your performance. Implement key performance indicators (KPIs) to monitor your progress and assess the efficiency of your operations. Regularly examine data and analytics to discover opportunities for improvement and optimization. Use this information to make informed decisions and modify your operations as needed to meet your development goals. By regularly monitoring and assessing your performance, you can identify areas for improvement and ensure that your operations are in line with your company's objectives.

Scaling your operations also entails creating a culture of innovation and continual improvement within your consulting firm. Encourage your team members to discuss ideas, try new ways, and challenge the status quo in order to foster innovation and progress. Create a supportive atmosphere in which team members feel encouraged to take chances, learn from their mistakes, and seek innovative solutions to business difficulties. Fostering an innovative culture can open up new chances for development and uniqueness in your consulting organization.

Also, as you expand your activities, it is critical to retain a focus on quality and client happiness. Prioritize providing high-quality services and surpassing client expectations at all touchpoints. Invest in training and development programs to guarantee that your team members have the skills and knowledge required to provide excellent results to your clients. On a regular basis, solicit feedback from clients and use it to constantly improve your services and client experience. Prioritizing quality and client happiness can help you build a solid reputation, promote client loyalty, and increase referrals and repeat business.

You may need to consider increasing your physical presence or investing in infrastructure to support your operations. This might include leasing office space, acquiring equipment, or investing in IT infrastructure to meet your team's demands. Evaluate your existing and future space and infrastructure needs, and make targeted investments to meet your development goals. Investing in the correct infrastructure, you can provide a friendly and productive work environment for your team while also positioning your company for long-term success.

Growing your business necessitates rigorous financial management and planning to ensure long-term success. To help you achieve your growth goals, continuously monitor your financial performance, analyze spending, and efficiently manage cash flow. Create a realistic budget and financial predictions that reflect your growth objectives and sales ambitions. Seek counsel from financial professionals or consultants to help you build a solid financial strategy and manage your funds responsibly as your activities grow.

Finally, as you expand your operations, it is critical to be nimble and adaptive to changes in the market and business environment. Prepare to shift your strategy, alter your operations, and grab new possibilities as they occur. Keep up with industry developments, technology development, and changes in customer wants and preferences, and be proactive in modifying your company strategy accordingly. Staying nimble and adaptive allows you to overcome problems, capitalize on opportunities, and sustain long-term success in your consulting firm.

Scaling your operations is a multifaceted process that includes optimizing processes, leveraging technology, assembling a strong team, encouraging innovation, prioritizing quality and client satisfaction, investing in infrastructure, managing finances responsibly, and remaining agile and adaptable. By implementing a planned and holistic approach to expanding your operations, you can efficiently fulfill rising demand for your services, promote sustainable development, and achieve long-term success in your consulting career. With careful planning, execution, and a dedication to continuous improvement, you may effectively grow your business and reach your full potential as a consultant.

Navigating the Consulting Industry

Starting a career in consulting necessitates a thorough awareness of the ever-changing world, a strategic attitude, and an unrelenting dedication to continual learning. Tracing the consulting market is analogous to traversing a large and ever-changing sea, where success is dependent on your ability to manage the currents, weather the storms, and chart a route that matches your professional goals.

Diversity is one of the consulting industry's distinguishing traits. Consultants work in a variety of industries, solving difficulties encountered by customers ranging from small firms to major organizations. Understanding this variety is critical because it helps you modify your approach, realizing that each customer and industry has distinct peculiarities that necessitate customized solutions.

As you traverse the consulting environment, gaining a thorough grasp of your chosen expertise becomes increasingly important. Typically, specialization is the compass that directs your path. Whether you discover your specialization in management, technology, healthcare, or another field, your knowledge forms the foundation of your value proposition. It is the lighthouse that attracts clients looking for your distinctive thoughts and solutions.

In the vast sea of consulting, networking creates an archipelago. Building and developing professional ties can help move your career ahead. Attend industry events, participate in online forums, and seek guidance from experienced experts. The contacts you make not only broaden your knowledge but can also lead to new possibilities and partnerships.

In the consulting sector, flexibility is the wind in your sails. The corporate landscape is ever-changing, shaped by technological breakthroughs, economic upheavals, and global events. Being aware of these changes enables you to alter your strategy accordingly, stay ahead of trends, and proactively tackle emerging difficulties.

Effective communication is the vehicle through which you convey your knowledge to clients. As a consultant, your ability to communicate complicated concepts clearly and compellingly is a valuable advantage. Cultivate excellent communication skills, both written and verbal, because they are the sails that attract new clients and stakeholders.

Establishing a strong reputation is the beacon that directs clients to your services. Consistently providing high-quality work, meeting deadlines, and surpassing expectations help to build a great reputation. Client testimonials, case studies, and a strong internet presence help to strengthen your industry reputation.

To stay on the cutting edge, adopt a constant learning attitude as the compass. The consulting sector is defined by fast change, so remaining current on the newest methodologies, technologies, and industry trends is critical. To keep your skills relevant, pursue professional development opportunities, continue your education, and seek mentoring.

Ethical navigation is the compass that will guide you through the consulting profession with integrity. Maintain ethical standards in all dealings with clients, coworkers, and stakeholders. Trust is the basis of effective consulting partnerships, and having a reputation for honesty and integrity is essential.

Staying current on industry trends

In the fast-paced and ever-changing world of consulting, being current on industry trends is not just a suggestion but a necessity for success. Your ability to predict industry developments, comprehend emerging technologies, and detect changing client demands as a consultant is critical to providing useful and relevant solutions. As you begin your consulting career, here are some tips to stay ahead of the curve and up-to-date on industry trends.

Develop the habit of continual learning. Make it a point to spend time each week reading industry-related information such as articles, research reports, white papers, and case studies. Follow credible industry journals, blogs, and thought leaders on social media to remain up-to-date on the newest advancements, best practices, and thought leadership in your area of expertise. Immersing yourself in industry-specific literature, you may obtain a better awareness of current trends and important insights to enhance your consulting approach.

Attend industry conferences, seminars, and networking events to broaden your knowledge and connect with colleagues and professionals in your sector. These events provide an important opportunity to learn from industry experts, participate in thought-provoking debates, and become acquainted with cutting-edge technology and processes. Take advantage of seminars, panel discussions, and keynote speeches to extend your viewpoint and remain current on industry trends that will shape the future of consulting.

Take advantage of professional development possibilities such as online courses, webinars, and seminars provided by respected organizations and universities. These learning experiences offer structured and targeted instruction on certain subjects or skills applicable to your consulting career. Whether it's mastering a new technology, learning about future market trends, or polishing your consulting abilities, investing in professional development ensures that you're prepared to meet your customers' changing demands and remain competitive in the consulting sector.

Aggressively solicit comments and ideas from your clients, coworkers, and industry peers. Regularly engage with your customers to learn about their difficulties, goals, and priorities and request feedback on your consulting services. Participate in discussions with colleagues and peers to trade ideas, share experiences, and learn from one another's achievements and mistakes. By carefully listening to the viewpoints of people in your industry environment, you may obtain significant insights into new trends, market dynamics, and client expectations that will help you shape your consulting business.

Use digital tools and resources to stay current on market developments in an efficient manner. Subscribe to industry-specific newsletters, set up Google Alerts for relevant keywords, and utilize social media monitoring tools to track conversations and topics in your area of expertise. Discover online groups and forums where experts in your business can share ideas, ask questions, and debate current trends. By embracing technology, you can have access to a variety of information and stay up-to-date on industry changes in real time, allowing you to tailor your consulting strategy accordingly.

Cultivate a sense of inquiry and flexibility. Approach your consulting profession with an open mind and a readiness to try new ideas, technology, and processes. Be proactive in your search for ways to learn and grow, and view change as a chance for creativity and growth. By cultivating a curious and adaptable attitude, you can remain nimble and sensitive to changing market trends, establishing yourself as a trusted adviser and thought leader in your field of expertise.

Being current on industry developments is critical for success in the consulting sector. You can stay ahead of the curve and informed about the latest developments shaping the future of consulting by cultivating a habit of continuous learning, attending industry events, engaging in professional development, seeking feedback and insights, leveraging technology tools, and adopting a curious and adaptable mindset. As you embark on your consulting career, commit to staying informed, curious, and adaptable to effectively navigate the ever-changing consulting world.

Developing Strategies To Effectively Compete In The Market

In the competitive consulting world, learning how to cope with competition is critical to success. As you begin your career as a consultant, you must understand that competition is not only unavoidable, but it also serves as a stimulus for innovation and progress. Adopting a strategic mentality and implementing tried-and-true strategies, you can manage the challenges of competition and position yourself for long-term success in the consulting sector.

One of the first stages in dealing with competition is undertaking extensive research to better understand your rivals. Determine who they are, what services they provide, their strengths and shortcomings, and their intended market. Understanding your rivals' strategy and positioning allows you to better analyze your own strengths and areas for distinction. This information enables you to properly position yourself in the market and personalize your services to the specific requirements of your target audience.

Work on developing a distinct value proposition that distinguishes you from the competition. Consider what distinguishes you from other consultants in your sector, and highlight these differences in your marketing materials, client interactions, and branding. Whether it's your specific knowledge, creative approach, or great customer service, clearly expressing your value proposition allows you to stand out in a competitive market and attract clients who understand your unique offering.

Furthermore, focus on developing great connections with your clients based on trust, openness, and dependability. Foster open communication, pay close attention to your clients' demands, and demonstrate your dedication to producing outcomes. By delivering outstanding service and developing a reputation for dependability and honesty, you may foster long-term relationships with clients that can resist competitive pressures.

In addition, use your network and professional contacts to broaden your reach and open up new chances. To broaden your area of influence, form alliances with complementary service providers, cooperate on collaborative initiatives with industry colleagues, and actively participate in networking events. By tapping into your network, you may obtain access to new customers, recommendations, and prospective partnerships that will help you remain competitive in the consulting market.

Stay up-to-date on industry trends, developing technology, and changing customer demands in order to remain nimble and adaptive in a competitive market. To keep ahead of the competition, invest in your professional development on a regular basis, attend industry events, and engage in continuous learning. Staying aware and proactive allows you to anticipate market developments and position yourself to take advantage of new possibilities when they arise.

Maintain a positive attitude and view competition as a source of innovation and success. Rather than perceiving rivals as dangers, see them as motivators to always grow and adapt. Adopt a growth mentality, see problems as opportunities for learning and development, and persevere in the face of setbacks. By tackling competition with a positive mindset and a dedication to continual development, you can transform problems into opportunities and prosper in the competitive consulting market.

It is important to regularly monitor and evaluate your competitors' strategies and market positioning. Monitor their actions, assess customer interactions, and analyze their marketing strategies.

Paying attention to your rivals' activities, you can spot potential dangers and opportunities, alter your own plans, and stay ahead of the competition.

Ensure that you consistently provide exceptional quality and value to your clients. Strive to exceed expectations on every project and provide solutions that truly benefit your clients' businesses. By consistently producing high-quality work and demonstrating your expertise, you can establish a strong reputation that distinguishes you from competitors and attracts clients looking for superior service and results.

In addition, work on developing a strong personal brand that connects with your target audience and sets you apart from competitors. Invest in creating a strong online presence with your website, social media profiles, and professional networks. To increase your industry's credibility and visibility, share valuable content, demonstrate your expertise, and engage with your audience. By cultivating a strong personal brand, you can attract clients who share your values and consulting approach.

Finally, remember that competition can lead to opportunities for collaboration and partnership. Instead of viewing other consultants as adversaries, consider how you can work together for mutual benefit.

Investigate opportunities for strategic alliances, joint ventures, and partnerships that combine each other's strengths and resources to provide more value to clients. By cultivating a collaborative and cooperative spirit, you can create win-win situations that benefit all parties involved while also keeping you competitive in the consulting industry.

Continuing professional development is essential

Starting a career as a consultant is the beginning of a lifelong journey of professional growth and development. In an ever-changing business landscape, professional development is not just a recommendation but a requirement for remaining competitive and relevant in the consulting industry. A commitment to continuous learning, skill development, and personal growth enables consultants to adapt to changing market dynamics, embrace new technologies, and provide exceptional value to their clients.

Professional development encompasses a diverse set of activities and initiatives aimed at improving both technical and soft skills. It entails staying current with industry trends, expanding knowledge in specific areas of expertise, improving communication and interpersonal skills, and developing leadership abilities. Consultants who invest in professional development can remain agile and adaptable, positioning themselves as trusted advisors capable of effectively meeting their clients' changing needs and challenges.

Staying up-to-date on industry trends and best practices is an important part of continuing professional development. Consultants must actively seek out opportunities to learn about the emerging trends, new technologies, and innovative methodologies that are influencing their industry. This can include attending industry conferences, seminars, and workshops, taking webinars and online courses, and connecting with thought leaders and experts in their field through networking events and professional associations.

Furthermore, continuing education and skill development are critical components of professional growth. Consultants should constantly seek ways to broaden their knowledge and expertise in their chosen field or niche. This could include pursuing advanced degrees or certifications, receiving specialized training in new technologies or methodologies, or participating in mentorship and coaching programs to improve their skills and capabilities.

In addition to technical skills, consultants must work to improve their soft skills, such as communication, negotiation, and leadership abilities.

Effective communication is essential for developing strong client relationships, presenting ideas persuasively, and working with colleagues and stakeholders. Negotiation skills are useful for navigating complex client engagements and reaching mutually beneficial agreements. Leadership skills are essential for inspiring and motivating team members, moving projects forward, and cultivating an innovative and excellence-oriented culture within organizations.

Continuing to develop professionally is critical to establishing a successful consulting career. Consultants can position themselves as trusted advisors who provide exceptional value to their clients by staying up-to-date on industry trends, constantly expanding their knowledge and expertise, honing technical and soft skills, and taking a proactive approach to learning and development. As consultants embark on their careers, they must view professional development as a lifelong commitment to excellence and continuous improvement.

Consultation ethics and professionalism

Ethics and professionalism will guide your interactions, decisions, and relationships with clients, colleagues, and stakeholders. Ethics and professionalism are more than just boxes to check or rules to follow; they are the basis upon which your reputation, credibility, and success as a consultant rest.

Ethics in consulting refers to a set of moral principles and ideals that guide how consultants should behave themselves in their professional responsibilities. It entails maintaining high levels of integrity, honesty, and openness in all dealings with customers and stakeholders. This includes delivering accurate and factual information, keeping confidentiality, and avoiding conflicts of interest that might jeopardize the quality of your job.

Furthermore, ethical consulting requires consultants to prioritize their clients' best interests above anything else. This entails working with a feeling of duty and obligation to provide value-added services that meet or exceed client expectations. Consultants must approach their job with a focus on quality, professionalism, and excellence, seeking to create concrete outcomes that help their customers' companies and objectives.

Professionalism in consulting is synonymous with ethics and comprises a variety of actions and characteristics that demonstrate consultants' commitment to their profession and their clients. It entails showing respect, civility, and honesty in all contacts, whether with clients, coworkers, or other stakeholders. Professionalism also includes a dedication to constant improvement and learning, as well as the ability to adapt to changing customer demands and market conditions.

Consultants must also maintain a high level of accountability for their activities and judgments. This includes accepting responsibility for their job, admitting mistakes, and working proactively to address any faults or deficiencies. Consultants should communicate with customers in a transparent manner, offering regular updates on project progress, difficulties encountered, and offered solutions.

Ethics and professionalism in consulting apply to the whole consulting organization, not just individual consultants. Consulting businesses must have clear rules and processes to encourage ethical behavior and professionalism among their staff. This may involve offering ethical decision-making training and guidance, putting in place methods for reporting unethical activity, and cultivating an organization-wide culture of integrity and responsibility.

In addition to ethical issues, professionalism in consulting includes good communication and interpersonal skills. This entails the ability to actively listen to clients' needs and problems, communicate effectively and concisely, and establish rapport and trust with them and others. Effective communication promotes cooperation, understanding, and guarantees that consultants can produce solutions that are in line with their customers' objectives.

Ethics and professionalism are fundamental concepts that guide consultants' behavior and activities in fulfilling their professional responsibilities. Consultants may develop a good reputation, acquire their clients' confidence, and achieve long-term success in their consulting professions by adhering to high ethical standards, exhibiting professionalism in all interactions, and putting their customers' best interests first. As you begin your career as a consultant, remember that ethics and professionalism are not optional; they are critical foundations that underpin your credibility, integrity, and effectiveness as a consultant.

Upholding Ethical Standards.

Ethical principles are the foundation of the consulting profession, governing consultants' dealings with clients, colleagues, and stakeholders. Preserving ethical standards is more than just a legal or regulatory necessity; it is an essential component of preserving trust, credibility, and integrity in the consulting sector.

It is critical that you grasp the value of ethical behavior and how it affects your reputation and the success of your consulting firm.

Upholding ethical standards entails following a set of moral principles and ideals that guide your behavior and decision-making processes.

Honesty and transparency are key elements of ethical consulting. Consultants must give their clients precise and genuine information without embellishments or misrepresentations that might lead to misunderstandings or poor judgments. Being open about your skills, expertise, and talents is critical for establishing trust and confidence with your clients.

Confidentiality is another essential component of ethical consultation. Consultants frequently have access to confidential information on their customers' businesses, strategies, and operations. Respecting and safeguarding the security of sensitive information is crucial to preventing unauthorized sharing or personal use. Clear confidentiality agreements and regulations can help consultants maintain this ethical standard while still providing significant insights and recommendations to their customers.

Avoiding conflicts of interest is also critical for ethical consulting. Consultants must put their clients' interests over their own and avoid engaging in actions that may jeopardize their neutrality or independence. This includes refusing to accept gifts or favors from clients, disclosing any potential conflicts of interest to clients upfront, and recusing oneself from activities that may involve a conflict of interest.

Ethical consultants also dedicate themselves to improving their customers' businesses and aiming for value-added services. This entails behaving with a sense of duty and obligation to produce high-quality work, fulfill deadlines, and accomplish predetermined results. Consultants must avoid overpromising and underdelivering, properly manage client expectations, and communicate clearly about project scope, dates, and deliverables.

In addition to client contacts, ethical consultants evaluate the overall influence of their job on society and the environment. Throughout their consulting engagements, they seek to reduce unfavorable externalities while maximizing beneficial results. This may include incorporating sustainability ideas into their suggestions, encouraging diversity and inclusion in their clients' businesses, and advocating for ethical business practices.

Ethical consultant commits to continuous self-reflection and progress. They routinely evaluate their own behavior and decision-making processes, soliciting input from customers, colleagues, and mentors to discover areas for improvement and development. Consultants may maintain an ethical and productive consulting practice by establishing a culture of continual learning and self-improvement.

Consultants must also be aware of the power dynamics that underpin consulting partnerships. Consultants hold influence and authority over their customers, who may rely on their knowledge and suggestions when making key business choices.

Consultants must use their influence appropriately, operate in the best interests of their clients, and refrain from any behaviors that may exploit or manipulate their clients' confidence.

Ethical consultants promote diversity, fairness, and inclusion in their consulting practices. They understand the significance of creating a diverse and inclusive work environment that respects and honors the viewpoints and contributions of all people. Consultants actively promote diversity and inclusion inside their client businesses, pushing for fair policies and practices that foster a more inclusive workplace culture.

In their consulting engagements, ethical consultants adhere to social responsibility and sustainability concepts. They assess the larger societal and environmental implications of their suggestions, with the goal of encouraging ethical corporate practices that promote good social transformation and environmental stewardship. Consultants may advise businesses on how to implement sustainable business strategies, reduce their environmental impact, and promote corporate social responsibility programs.

Managing Conflicts of Interest

One of the most important ethical issues for a consultant is how to resolve conflicts of interest. Conflicts of interest occur when your personal interests or affiliations clash with your professional responsibilities or commitments to your clients. These conflicts can develop in a variety of scenarios, including when you have a personal relationship with a client, a financial stake in a client's business, or conflicting duties to many clients.

Effective conflict of interest management necessitates a dedication to openness, ethics, and putting your clients' best interests first. When confronted with a possible conflict of interest, it is critical to inform all parties concerned and take the necessary steps to limit the impact on your ability to give objective and unbiased advice.

First and foremost, consultants must detect conflicts of interest and analyze the possible impact on their ability to perform their professional tasks. This necessitates a full grasp of the nature of the disagreement and its consequences for the consulting project. Consultants should assess the gravity of the dispute, the possible risks and advantages, as well as the ethical implications of their decisions.

Consultants must notify all relevant parties, including their clients and any other stakeholders involved in the consulting engagement, when they discover a conflict of interest. Full disclosure promotes openness and empowers customers to make educated decisions about how to proceed. Consultants must disclose clear and accurate information on the nature of the conflict, its possible influence on the consulting engagement, and any actions taken to reduce its impacts.

In addition to disclosure, consultants must take proactive measures to reduce the impact of the conflict of interest on their capacity to give objective and unbiased advice. This may include recusing oneself from specific areas of the consulting engagement, seeking advice from colleagues or mentors, or putting in place measures to ensure that the conflict does not jeopardize the work's quality or integrity.

Consultants must avoid circumstances in which their personal interests or affiliations may have an undue impact on their professional judgment or decisions. This may necessitate establishing boundaries and clear guidelines for managing potential conflicts of interest, such as refraining from engaging in activities that could result in a perceived or actual conflict of interest or seeking approval from clients or other stakeholders before acting.

Effective conflict-of-interest management necessitates a commitment to ethical behavior, openness, and responsibility. Consultants can maintain their clients' trust and confidence while upholding the highest standards of integrity in their consulting practice by recognizing conflicts of interest, disclosing them to all affected parties, taking proactive steps to mitigate their impact, and avoiding situations where conflicts may jeopardize their professional judgment. As you begin your consulting career, keep in mind that ethical behavior is more than a requirement; it is a basic value that informs your interactions, decisions, and relationships with clients and stakeholders.

Ensuring Client Confidentiality.

In the consulting industry, maintaining client confidentiality is not just a legal requirement but also a foundation of trust and professionalism. As a consultant, you have access to sensitive information about your clients' businesses, plans, and operations, and it is your job to protect this information with the utmost care and discretion.

Client confidentiality is critical for building trust and positive relationships with your clients. When customers share sensitive information with you, they expect you to keep it secret and only use it to provide them with the best advice and solutions available.

To preserve client confidentiality, consultants must develop explicit norms and processes for handling sensitive material. This involves putting in place strong data security measures to prevent unauthorized access or exposure of customer information, such as encryption, secure data storage systems, and access restrictions.

Consultants must follow any confidentiality or non-disclosure agreements (NDAs) they have signed with their clients. These agreements legally bind consultants to keep client information secret and restrict them from revealing or utilizing it for purposes other than the consulting engagement.

In addition to safeguarding client information from external risks, consultants must also be aware of internal threats to client confidentiality. This involves ensuring that all employees and contractors are aware of their client confidentiality duties, as well as giving training and guidance on how to safely handle private information.

Consultants must be prepared to respond quickly and efficiently in the event of a data breach or unlawful exposure of client information. This may include contacting impacted clients, determining the source of the breach, and adopting corrective actions to prevent future instances.

Keeping client confidentiality is critical to establishing and growing a successful consulting profession. Consultants can increase trust, credibility, and integrity in their consulting practice by establishing clear protocols and procedures for dealing with confidential information, exercising discretion and good judgment in communications and interactions, adhering to confidentiality agreements, and responding effectively to breaches or unauthorized disclosures. As you begin your consulting career, keep in mind that client confidentiality is more than simply a legal obligation; it is a pillar of trust and professionalism that serves as the foundation for your client interactions.

Manage your consulting career

Consider beginning a trip into the world of consulting, where every decision you make and move you take influences the course of your career. Managing your consulting career is more than just finding chances and climbing the corporate ladder; it's about carving out a path that resonates with your passions, values, and objectives while navigating the consulting industry's ever-changing landscape.

At the core of managing your consulting career is the desire for constant growth and development. Investing in your skills, knowledge, and expertise can help you stay ahead of the curve and compete in a fast-changing market. Whether you're pursuing advanced certifications, attending industry conferences, or looking for mentoring possibilities, continuous learning is essential for broadening your professional horizons and opening doors to new prospects.

Equally it is crucial to be developing a solid professional network that may help move your career ahead. Networking is more than just exchanging business cards and connecting on LinkedIn; it is about developing real connections with coworkers, mentors, and industry peers who can provide direction, counsel, and possibilities for cooperation. By cultivating these relationships and actively engaging in professional networks, you may have access to a plethora of knowledge and tools that can help you manage the ups and downs of your consulting career.

Managing your consulting career demands a thorough awareness of market trends and industry dynamics. The consulting environment is continually changing, with new technology, processes, and market factors affecting the delivery and consumption of consulting services. Staying current with these trends and responding to changing market situations is critical for being relevant and competitive in business. Furthermore, efficient time management and prioritizing are critical abilities for navigating your consulting job. As a consultant, you may be juggling many projects, clients, and deadlines at the same time, necessitating careful balancing of conflicting demands and the allocation of time and resources. By mastering time management strategies and establishing clear priorities, you may increase your productivity and focus on things that will have the most influence on your career.

In addition to controlling your workload, it's critical to maintain a healthy work-life balance. The consulting industry is recognized for its rigorous schedules and high-pressure conditions, which may have a negative impact on your physical and mental health if not handled appropriately. Prioritizing self-care, setting boundaries, and taking time to recharge are critical for preserving your overall health and happiness while pursuing a rewarding consulting job.

Finally, managing your consulting career entails establishing long-term goals and making aggressive efforts to attain them. Whether you want to be a leader in your business, create your own consulting practice, or specialize in a certain area or specialty, having a clear vision for your career path may give you guidance and drive as you navigate your professional journey.

Setting Goals and Milestones.

Imagine yourself standing on the brink of huge and undiscovered terrain, ready to begin a journey towards your hopes and goals. Setting objectives and milestones is similar to charting a course across this terrain, directing you on a road of success, achievement, and contentment in your consulting profession.

Setting goals entails more than simply visualizing where you want to go; it also entails constructing a road map outlining the measures you must take to get there. Setting clear and achievable objectives, whether it's getting your dream job at a prominent consulting company, becoming an expert in a certain area or specialty, or launching your own consulting business, gives your career path emphasis and direction.

Furthermore, objectives act as sources of motivation and inspiration, boosting your drive and desire to conquer barriers and endure in the face of adversity.

They provide you with something to strive for, aspire to, and rejoice in when you reach your goals. Each objective you establish serves as a milestone along the route of your consulting career, indicating development and accomplishment.

Setting goals, however, is more than just dreaming big; it also requires deliberate and practical planning. This is breaking down your larger goals into smaller, more attainable tasks or milestones that you may work toward progressively. These milestones act as checkpoints throughout your trip, allowing you to monitor your progress and change direction as needed.

Creating explicit and quantifiable goals clarifies your goals and establishes a clear bar for success. Instead of broad desires like "I want to be successful in my consulting career," adopting SMART goals—specific, measurable, realistic, relevant, and time-bound—allows you to define success and provide clear criteria for completion.

Defining objectives necessitates introspection and self-awareness, as you evaluate not just what you want to accomplish but also why it is important to you. Understanding your motives and values may help you develop meaningful goals that are in line with your personal and professional objectives. It's about figuring out what you enjoy doing, what you're excellent at, and what the world needs, and then developing objectives based on that intersection.

In addition to creating individual goals, it is important to define long-term professional objectives and a vision for your consulting career as a whole. This entails picturing where you want to go in five, ten, or twenty years and establishing overall goals that are consistent with that vision. With a clear sense of direction and purpose, you can make purposeful decisions and perform deliberate activities that will get you closer to your long-term goals.

Furthermore, creating goals and milestones allows you to take charge of your consulting career and actively determine its direction. Rather than waiting for chances to present themselves, defining objectives allows you to actively seek out new experiences, acquire new abilities, and pursue opportunities that correspond with your goals.

Setting objectives also instills a sense of accountability and responsibility, making you accountable to yourself and your aims. Setting defined targets and deadlines fosters a sense of urgency and dedication to taking action and making progress toward your goals. This responsibility drives your ambition and tenacity, encouraging you to remain focused and disciplined in your quest for achievement.

Balancing work and personal life.

As a consultant, navigating the exciting yet challenging world of professional consulting. As you begin on this road, you rapidly find that juggling business and personal life is a delicate tightrope walk that takes skill, resilience, and intentionality.

Consulting is known for its demanding schedules, strict deadlines, and high-pressure conditions. It is a job that requires your complete attention and concentration, sometimes blurring the barriers between work and personal life. However, striking a good balance between the two is critical for your overall health, happiness, and long-term success as a consultant.

Setting limits and prioritizing tasks are the first steps toward achieving balance. It's about understanding that, while your job is vital, so are your personal connections, health, and general well-being. Setting clear boundaries around your work hours, responsibilities, and availability frees up time for you to recharge, relax, and engage in things that offer you joy and fulfillment away from work.

Efficient time management is required to balance work and personal life as a consultant. With so many projects, clients, and deadlines vying for your attention, it's easy to become overwhelmed and stretched thin. However, by prioritizing tasks, making realistic objectives, and scheduling time for both professional and personal activities, you may increase your productivity and guarantee that you have time for the things that are most important to you.

In addition to time management, it is critical to develop self-care activities that promote your physical, mental, and emotional well-being. This may include regular exercise, a nutritious diet, mindfulness techniques, and enough rest and relaxation. Self-care is not a luxury; it is essential for sustaining your energy, attention, and resilience in the face of professional demands.

Honest communication with coworkers, clients, and loved ones is critical for balancing work and personal life. By properly stating your limits, requirements, and priorities, you may manage expectations and prevent overcommitting to work at the expense of your personal life. Furthermore, seeking assistance from coworkers, mentors, and loved ones may provide you with vital guidance, perspective, and encouragement as you negotiate the obstacles of juggling work and personal life.

Finding methods to merge your professional and personal lives might help you live a more balanced and satisfying life as a consultant. Rather than perceiving them as distinct entities fighting for your time and attention, think about how you may connect your professional obligations with your personal goals and beliefs.

For example, you may look at ways to incorporate aspects of your personal life into your business, such as seeking consultancy assignments that correspond with your interests or ideals. Working on projects that speak to you on a personal level allows you to discover more happiness and purpose in your career while also cultivating your personal interests.

Similarly, incorporating parts of your profession into your personal life might help you feel more balanced and fulfilled. This might be sharing your consulting project experiences and insights with friends and family or contributing your professional skills and knowledge to causes or organizations that are important to you outside of work.

Continuous Learning And Growth.

Entering the dynamic and ever-changing world of consulting. From the minute you begin this path, you realize that ongoing learning and improvement are not just advised but required for success and longevity in your work. your success is dependent on your ability to adapt to shifting trends, technology, and client requirements. This necessitates a dedication to lifelong learning and development, a spirit of curiosity and inquiry, and a readiness to accept new challenges and possibilities.

Continuous learning is more than just gaining new skills or information; it is about fostering a growth mindset that supports a lifetime love of learning and development. It's about seeing every project, client encounter, and difficulty as a chance to increase your horizons, enhance your knowledge, and widen your viewpoint.

In the fast-paced world of consulting, being current and competitive entails staying ahead of the curve and up-to-date on the latest industry trends, best practices, and emerging technology. This might include visiting industry conferences, workshops, and seminars, obtaining further certifications or degrees, or participating in online courses and self-study programs.

Continuous learning extends beyond technical skills and industry knowledge to include soft skills like communication, leadership, problem-solving, and emotional intelligence. As a consultant, your success is dependent not just on your knowledge but also on your ability to communicate, cooperate, and lead others.

It goes beyond official training and education to encompass informal learning opportunities like mentorship, coaching, and peer-to-peer learning. By searching out mentors and coaches who can provide direction, feedback, and support, you may speed your learning and growth while also gaining useful insights from their experiences. Adopting a culture of continual learning and growth necessitates a willingness to venture outside of your comfort zone and accept new tasks and responsibilities. It's about accepting uncertainty, seeing failure as a chance for progress, and using feedback as a driver for change.

Continual learning and growth are more than simply methods for success in your consulting career; they are critical components of a rewarding and meaningful professional journey. Adopting a lifelong learning mentality, committing to personal and professional development, and grabbing chances for growth and development, you may realize your full potential as a consultant and succeed in the dynamic and fulfilling world of consulting.

Conclusion

Finally, pursuing a career as a consultant is an exciting and fulfilling path that offers opportunities for growth, learning, and professional development. Throughout this thorough book, we have looked at the key procedures, tactics, and abilities required to effectively traverse the world of consulting.

From learning the fundamentals of consulting and honing your skills to developing a strong personal brand and establishing your presence in the industry, each section of this guide has been designed to provide you with the knowledge, tools, and insights you need to succeed in your consulting career.

We've looked at how to create objectives, manage projects, and deal with problems while keeping a good work-life balance and adhering to ethical guidelines. Furthermore, we have stressed the significance of constant learning, growth, and flexibility as critical components of success in the dynamic and ever-changing consulting industry.

As you begin your career as a consultant, remember that success is more than simply attaining your professional objectives; it is also about finding fulfillment and balance in other parts of your life. By adopting a mentality of inquiry, resilience, and lifelong learning, you can negotiate the complexity of the consulting profession with confidence, honesty, and a dedication to quality.

In essence, this guide is a road map to assist you in navigating the fascinating and tough world of consulting, allowing you to design your route, overcome barriers, and reach your full potential as a consultant. As you begin on this road, remember that success is not always simple, but with effort, patience, and a desire to learn, you may carve yourself a satisfying and rewarding career in the consulting industry.

Final thoughts

In the ever-changing world of consulting, pursuing a career in this dynamic sector offers a path full of challenges, chances, and progress. As you consider the extensive insights and methods offered in this guide, keep in mind that success in consulting requires more than just technical competence or industry knowledge.

At its foundation, success in consulting requires a mindset of continual learning, adaptation, and resilience. It is about developing genuine client connections, keeping ethical standards, and providing outstanding value on each assignment. It is about striking a balance between professional ambition and personal fulfillment, supporting both your work goals and your overall well-being.

As you negotiate the complexity of the consulting profession, remember to be true to your principles, operate with integrity in all relationships, and be open to new challenges and chances for advancement. Accept every encounter as an opportunity to learn, innovate, and make a positive difference in the businesses and industries you serve.

Above all, remember that your experience as a consultant is unique to you, and there is no one-size-fits-all route to success. Be courageous in pursuing your objectives, seek out mentors and allies to help you along the road, and never underestimate the power of perseverance and dedication.

As you embark on your journey into the fascinating world of consulting, may this book be a great resource and source of inspiration as you strive to achieve your goals and make a lasting influence in your profession and beyond.

Next Steps on Your Consulting Journey

As you wrap up this thorough guide on establishing a career as a consultant, it's critical to consider the next stages in your consulting path. With your knowledge, methods, and insights, you are ready to act and go on a road of professional progress and success.

1. **Reflect on your objectives:** Take some time to consider your professional objectives and aspirations. Clarify your goals as a consultant and what success means for you in the short and long term.

2. **Develop a strategy:** Based on your objectives, establish a tailored strategy outlining the measures you must take to grow your consulting profession. Consider topics including skill development, networking possibilities, and project acquisition tactics.

3. **Continuous Learning:** Commit to ongoing learning and professional growth. Attending workshops, seminars, and conferences allows you to stay up-to-date on industry trends, emerging technology, and best consulting practices. Seek mentoring and coaching opportunities to improve your skills and knowledge.

4. Network: Develop and cultivate ties within the consulting community. Attend networking events, join professional groups, and connect with colleagues and industry leaders both online and in person. Networking may lead to new possibilities, collaborations, and useful insights.

5. **Obtain experience:** Look for ways to obtain hands-on experience in consulting. Consider internships, part-time jobs, or volunteer activities to enhance your portfolio and skill set. Real-world experience is crucial for developing your consulting career.

6. **Market Yourself:** Create a strong personal brand and online presence to demonstrate your competence and attract prospective

clients or jobs. Create a professional website, use social media channels, and share your knowledge via blog entries, articles, or presentations.

7. **Seek input:** Gather input from mentors, coworkers, and clients to learn about your strengths and places for growth. Constructive comments may help you improve your abilities, boost your performance, and advance as a consultant.

8. **Stay Agile:** Maintain adaptability and flexibility in the face of changing circumstances and market trends. Accept new difficulties, grab chances for development, and be open to adjusting your strategy as needed to remain relevant and competitive in the consulting sector.

9. **Maintain Work-Life Balance:** Put your health first and endeavor to maintain a good work-life balance. Set limits, plan time for self-care and relaxation, and devote time to hobbies outside of work that offer you joy and fulfillment.

10. **Evaluate and Adjust:** Evaluate your progress toward your goals on a regular basis and adjust your strategy as appropriate. Be willing to review your priorities, refine your strategy, and seize new chances that correspond with your growing goals.

Completing the above steps, you may grow your consulting career, broaden your influence, and attain your professional objectives. Remember that your career as a consultant is a dynamic and continuing process, and each step you take puts you closer to reaching your full potential in this exciting and gratifying field.

Appendix:

Resources for further learning

As you end your research into establishing a career as a consultant, it's critical that you continue to broaden your knowledge and abilities through other resources. Here are some tips to help you continue your learning journey:

1. **Books:** Discover books published by professional consultants and industry experts to obtain a deeper understanding of various consulting topics. Look for titles that address corporate strategy, project management, client interactions, and consulting leadership.

2. **Online Courses:** Enroll in online courses provided by credible platforms and universities to improve your abilities in areas related to consulting. Consider courses in strategic consulting, data analysis, communication, and company growth.

3. Subscribe to industry periodicals, journals, and magazines that cover consulting and allied subjects. These publications frequently include essays, case studies, and interviews with industry professionals, which provide useful insights into current trends and best practices.

4. **Professional Associations:** Consultants can join professional associations and networking groups to interact with colleagues, attend events, and access resources such as webinars, whitepapers, and research reports. Participating in a network of fellow consultants may provide support, cooperation possibilities, and useful industry insights.

5. **Podcasts:** Listen to podcasts hosted by consultants and business leaders on themes such as consulting, entrepreneurship, leadership, and professional development. Podcasts are a great way to study on the fly and get varied viewpoints from industry leaders.

6. **Blogs and Websites:** Follow blogs and websites that offer consulting and business-advising services. These platforms frequently provide essays, case studies, and practical advice for consultants seeking to improve their abilities and expand their practices.

7. **Networking Events:** Attend industry conferences, workshops, and networking events to meet people in the consulting sector and other industries. These events provide an opportunity to learn from seasoned practitioners, share ideas, and broaden your professional network.

8. **Mentoring Programs:** Look for mentoring opportunities with experienced consultants who can offer direction, advice, and support as you go through your consulting career. Mentorship programs provided by professional groups or through informal networking may be extremely beneficial for career development.

Using these resources for additional learning, you may continue to improve your abilities, broaden your knowledge, and remain up-to-date on the newest trends and best practices in the consulting profession. Remember, learning is a lifetime process, and investing in your professional growth can help you succeed as a consultant.

Sample consulting agreements.

As your consulting career progresses, it is critical that you understand consulting agreements and contracts in order to protect your interests and guarantee a successful client engagement. While consulting agreements might differ depending on the exact nature of the project and client requirements, below are some major aspects often included in example consulting agreements:

1. Scope of Work: Clearly identify the consulting services that will be performed, including deliverables, milestones, and dates. Outline the exact duties, objectives, and outcomes you expect from the consultant.

2. Fees and Payment Terms: Detail the remuneration structure, including the consultant's fees, payment schedule, and any additional charges or reimbursement costs. Clarify payment arrangements, such as upfront deposits, installment payments, and milestone-based payments.

3. Confidentiality and Non-Disclosure: Make arrangements to safeguard the confidentiality of sensitive information given throughout the consulting engagement. Define the scope of secrecy, the parties' duties, and the processes for managing confidential information.

4. Intellectual Property Rights: Discuss the ownership and rights to any intellectual property generated or developed during the consulting engagement. Specify whether the consultant retains ownership of any work output or if it passes to the customer upon project completion.

5. Termination Clause: Describe the circumstances and processes for terminating the consulting agreement, such as grounds for termination, notice periods, and any related termination costs or

penalties.

6. Indemnification: Define both parties' obligations and liabilities in the event of a consulting engagement-related disagreement, claim, or legal action. Plan for indemnity and liability limits to protect both the consultant and the client.

7. Governing legislation and dispute resolution: Specify the legislation that governs the consulting agreement and define the processes for resolving any issues or disagreements between the parties. Consider incorporating provisions for mediation, arbitration, and other forms of alternative conflict resolution.

8. Insurance Requirements: Determine if the consultant must have professional liability insurance or any other forms of insurance coverage during the consulting contract. Specify the minimum coverage limits and any extra insured endorsements requested by the customer.

9. Party Relationship: Clarify the nature of the consultant-client relationship, emphasizing that the consultant is an independent contractor and not the client's employee or agent. Include safeguards that ensure the consultant's independence and autonomy while executing the services.

10. Miscellaneous Provisions: Include any extra terms or conditions applicable to the consulting engagement, such as confidentiality, non-solicitation of employees or clients, governing legislation, and revisions to the agreement.

When creating or reviewing consulting agreements, you should contact legal counsel or skilled experts to guarantee compliance with applicable laws and regulations, as well as to safeguard your rights and interests as a consultant. In addition, personalize the consulting agreement to the individual needs and requirements of each client and project to ensure a mutually productive and effective consulting partnership.

A Glossary of Consulting Terms.

As you learn more about consulting, it's crucial to become acquainted with the industry's main terms. Here's a dictionary of popular consulting phrases to help you manage discussions, papers, and interactions in the consulting field:

1. Consultant: A person or company engaged to give professional advice, solutions, and suggestions to customers regarding specific business difficulties or possibilities.

2. Client: The individual or organization that hires a consultant to solve a specific problem, achieve certain goals, or enhance company performance.

3. Engagement: A formal agreement or contract between a consultant and a client to offer consulting services within a certain scope of work, length, and price structure.

4. Scope of Work (SOW): A full explanation of the tasks, deliverables, and objectives that the consultant will complete throughout the engagement, including project limits and expectations.

5. Fee Structure: The remuneration structure between the consultant and the client, which includes the consultant's fees, payment arrangements, and any other charges or costs related to the engagement,.

6. Deliverable: A concrete deliverable or result created by the consultant during the consulting engagement, such as a report, presentation, strategy plan, or analysis.

7. Stakeholders: Individuals or groups interested in or influencing the consulting project, such as clients, employees, customers, suppliers,

regulators, and other relevant parties.

8. Requirements Assessment: A systematic method for identifying, assessing, and prioritizing an organization's or business's requirements, issues, and opportunities in order to choose where to focus consulting efforts.

9. SWOT Analysis: A framework for assessing an organization's strengths, weaknesses, opportunities, and threats, resulting in insights about its internal capabilities and external environment.

10. Benchmarking is the process of comparing an organization's performance, procedures, or measurements to those of rivals or industry peers in order to discover areas for improvement and best practices.

11. Change Management: The process of planning, implementing, and managing organizational change efforts to successfully transfer individuals, teams, and processes from their present state to a desired future one.

12. Risk management is the process of identifying, analyzing, and minimizing risks and uncertainties that may affect the success or consequences of a consulting project or organizational endeavor.

13. Value Proposition: A consultant's unique mix of goods, services, and perks tailored to the specific needs and requirements of their clients, highlighting the value they can provide.

14. ROI (Return on Investment): A metric for determining the financial returns or advantages of investing in a consulting project or effort in comparison to the expenditures paid.

15. Best Practices: established methods, strategies, or procedures that have been proven to be successful and efficient in attaining desired results or solving common business challenges in a certain industry or domain.

16. Key Performance Indicators (KPIs) are quantifiable metrics or indicators used to assess the performance, progress, and success of a consulting project or corporate endeavor against established goals and objectives.

17. Strategic Planning: The process of establishing an organization's purpose, vision, goals, and strategies to guide decision-making and resource allocation while ensuring alignment with long-term goals.

18. Business Process Improvement: A systematic strategy for discovering, assessing, and improving current business processes in order to improve an organization's efficiency, effectiveness, and value delivery.

19. Quality Assurance: A collection of activities and procedures that guarantee consultancy outputs satisfy predetermined standards, requirements, and client expectations while maintaining a high degree of quality and consistency.

20. Continuous Improvement: Is the continual endeavor to discover, implement, and sustain incremental adjustments and upgrades to consulting processes, methods, and outcomes in order to promote continuous learning and progress.

Knowing this consulting terminology can help you communicate more effectively, grasp project needs, and negotiate the complexities of consulting engagements with confidence and clarity.

www.ingramcontent.com/pod-product-compliance
Lightning Source LLC
Chambersburg PA
CBHW071056240526
45471CB00016B/1941